The Science and Law of School Segregation and Diversity

American Psychology-Law Society Series

Books in the Series

Trial Consulting
Amy J. Posey and Lawrence S. Wrightsman

Death by Design
Craig Haney

Psychological Injuries
William J. Koch, Kevin S. Douglas, Tonia L. Nicholls, and Melanie L. O'Neill

Emergency Department Treatment of the Psychiatric Patient
Susan Stefan

The Psychology of the Supreme Court
Lawrence S. Wrightsman

Proving the Unprovable
Christopher Slobogin

Adolescents, Media, and the Law
Roger J.R. Levesque

Oral Arguments Before the Supreme Court
Lawrence S. Wrightsman

God in the Courtroom
Brian H. Bornstein and Monica K. Miller

Expert Testimony on the Psychology of Eyewitness Identification
Edited by Brian L. Cutler

The Psychology of Judicial Decision-Making
Edited by David Klein and Gregory Mitchell

The Miranda Ruling: Its Past, Present, and Future
Lawrence S. Wrightsman and Mary L. Pitman

Juveniles at Risk: A Plea for Preventive Justice
Christopher Slobogin and Mark R. Fondacaro

The Ethics of Total Confinement
Bruce A. Arrigo, Heather Y. Bersot, and Brian G. Sellers

International Human Rights and Mental Disability Law
Michael L. Perlin

Applying Social Science to Reduce Violent Offending
Edited by Joel Dvoskin, Jennifer L. Skeem, Raymond W. Novaco, and Kevin S. Douglas

Children Who Resist Postseparation Parental Contact
Barbara Jo Fidler, Nicholas Bala, and Michael A. Saini

Trauma, Stress, and Wellbeing in the Legal System
Edited by Monica K. Miller and Brian H. Bornstein

Psychology, Law, and the Wellbeing of Children
Edited by Monica K. Miller, Jared C. Chamberlain, and Twila Wingrove

Murder in the Courtroom: The Cognitive Neuroscience of Extreme Violent Behavior
Brigitte Vallabhajosula

Rational Suicide, Irrational Laws: Examining Current Approaches to Suicide in Policy and Law
Susan Stefan

International Perspectives on Violence Risk Assessment
Edited by Jay P. Singh, Stål Bjørkly, and Seena Fazel

Adolescence, Privacy, and the Law: A Developmental Science Perspective
Roger J.R. Levesque

The Ethical Practice of Forensic Psychology: A Casebook
Edited by Gianni Pirelli, Robert A. Beattey, and Patricia A. Zapf

The Jury Under Fire: Myth, Controversy, and Reform
Brian H. Bornstein and Edie Greene

The Science and Law of School Segregation and Diversity
Roger J.R. Levesque

The Science and Law of School Segregation and Diversity

Roger J.R. Levesque

OXFORD
UNIVERSITY PRESS

OXFORD
UNIVERSITY PRESS

Oxford University Press is a department of the University of Oxford. It furthers the University's objective of excellence in research, scholarship, and education by publishing worldwide. Oxford is a registered trade mark of Oxford University Press in the UK and certain other countries.

Published in the United States of America by Oxford University Press
198 Madison Avenue, New York, NY 10016, United States of America.

Library of Congress Cataloging-in-Publication Data
Names: Levesque, Roger J. R., author.
Title: The science and law of school segregation and diversity / Roger J.R. Levesque.
Description: Oxford [UK] ; New York : Oxford University Press, [2018] |
Series: American Psychology-Law Society Series |
Includes bibliographical references and index.
Identifiers: LCCN 2017029919 (print) | LCCN 2017031362 (ebook) |
ISBN 9780190633646 (updf) | ISBN 9780190670030 (epub) | ISBN 9780190633639
Subjects: LCSH: Segregation in education—Law and legislation—United States. |
Educational equalization—Law and legislation—United States. |
Discrimination in education—Law and legislation—United States. |
United States—Race relations.
Classification: LCC KF4155 (ebook) | LCC KF4155 .L48 2017 (print) |
DDC 344.73/0798—dc23
LC record available at https://lccn.loc.gov/2017029919

Contents

Series Foreword

This book series is sponsored by the American Psychology-Law Society (APLS). APLS is an interdisciplinary organization devoted to scholarship, practice, and public service in psychology and law. Its goals include advancing the contributions of psychology to the understanding of law and legal institutions through basic and applied research; promoting the education of psychologists in matters of law and the education of legal personnel in matters of psychology; and informing the psychological and legal communities and the general public of current research, educational, and service activities in the field of psychology and law. APLS membership includes psychologists from the academic, research, and clinical practice communities as well as members of the legal community. Research and practice is represented in both the civil and criminal legal arenas. APLS has chosen Oxford University Press as a strategic partner because of its commitment to scholarship, quality, and the international dissemination of ideas. These strengths will help APLS reach its goal of educating the psychology and legal professions and the general public about important developments in psychology and law. The focus of the book series reflects the diversity of the field of psychology and law, as we will publish books on a broad range of topics.

In the latest book in the series, *The Science and Law of School Segregation and Diversity*, Roger Levesque, a legal scholar, explores the source, nature, and implications of disagreements about what constitutes segregation and related phenomena such as desegregation, integration, and discrimination. Through a detailed analysis of the two *Brown v. Board of Education* cases (1954, 1955), Levesque highlights disagreements about the issue of segregation and presents empirical analyses of these issues. Through the course of six chapters, Levesque lays the foundation for his analysis; examines the general parameters of how the legal system addresses claims alleging violation of rights, such as those involving differential treatment based on race; details how the legal system applies the legal developments to racial classifications; evaluates empirical evidence addressing two fundamental approaches to segregation and diversity (anti-classification and anti-subordination); expands the analysis to research related to the necessity of remedial approaches as well as potential alternatives; and completes the analysis with some, perhaps, surprising conclusions about the law and the empirical research in this domain.

The Science and Law of School Segregation and Diversity presents a comprehensive and detailed analysis of these important issues and leaves the reader with a better understanding of both legal and empirical foundations for segregation and diversity as well as the role of societal demands. Scholars, researchers, policymakers, and practitioners will undoubtedly find that this book has the potential to help shape the future of interactions with policy and the legal system.

Patricia A. Zapf
Series Editor

The Science and
Law of School Segregation and Diversity

1

The Dramatic Clarification of School Segregation and Diversity Law

The Spread of Contemporary Segregation

Educational segregation is spreading. Even in the South, the heart of the civil rights era's desegregation efforts, Black and Latino students now increasingly experience segregation from students of other racial and ethnic groups (Orfield & Frankenberg, 2014). In other areas of the country that historically were not segregated, educational segregation by race and ethnicity deepens as societal diversity increases. Even the suburbia of many large metropolitan areas—types of residential patterns less prominent during the civil rights era—now exhibit racial and ethnic segregation in their school systems. Throughout the nation, educational segregation is more rampant than at the initiation of the civil rights era's unprecedented movement toward equality, with estimates ranging from substantial increases to little change toward the better depending on the region and racial/ethnic groups (Reardon & Owens, 2014). Although rising percentages of different ethnic/racial and multiracial groups complicate statistical findings, Blacks still remain substantially more segregated from Whites than other racial/ethnic groups, despite the legacy of school desegregation and integration efforts targeted at Black youth (Stroub & Richards, 2013).

This vast segregation of the nation's schools is baffling. We live in a society in which segregation officially no longer exists. More than six decades ago, *Brown v. Board of Education* (1954, p. 495) concluded that schools that segregated youth by race were "inherently unequal" and rejected all policies that supported it. *Brown* overturned a policy of "separate but equal" that itself had lasted almost six decades under *Plessy v. Ferguson* (1896, p. 548). By concluding that separation hampered equality, *Brown* began the largest constitutional change ever to affect American education. In the end, *Brown* did more than officially end segregation; it spurred massive desegregation efforts and integration. Yet, segregation persists. Desegregation efforts are rapidly being abandoned. And the extent of integration efforts remains unknown.

Educational segregation continues largely for a simple reason. Segregation can describe different situations, but only one of them now matters to the legal system's approach to ensuring equality in primary and secondary schools. The Supreme Court now defines racial segregation as situations of racial imbalance due to the government's directly treating people differently on the basis of race (*Parents Involved in Community Schools v. Seattle School District No. 1*, 2007). The vast majority of segregation reported by commentators and experienced by youth simply does not qualify because that segregation is due to factors other than direct governmental mandates that require different treatment. The type of segregation identified by commentators derives from factors that the Court views as private decisions, such as those relating to residential patterns, financial status, family size, and individual preferences that influence where students live and attend school. Legally, if the government—through the legal system—does not directly mandate the use of race or ethnicity to determine school assignments, then there is no segregation.

The previous distinctions may appear like unfair legal technicalities, but they root firmly in how the legal system approaches discrimination law. The distinctions constitute the major distinction between *de jure* and *de facto* forms of discrimination. The former results from the government's mandate; the latter just happens without being directly compelled by the government. The former demands close scrutiny to ensure its legitimacy; the latter is presumed legitimate, as something outside of the government's formal control. The first must be stopped, or at least addressed by the government; the second can continue.

The narrow approach to addressing segregation—one based on de jure actions—has important repercussions. It means that the legal system no longer views government-supported discrimination as a widespread social ill that materially contributes to the production and maintenance of segregated spaces. It also means that the legal system no longer links discrimination to the harms of segregation. The government's lack of direct involvement means that segregation just does not exist, and something that does not exist cannot harm. This is not to say that particular situations could not be harmful. It is just that those situations do not create the types of harms that require a response from the legal system. In fact, the legal system typically cannot respond directly to those situations because its own actions would create legally impermissible harms if it were to use, for example, racial classifications to address them. In other words, adopting a narrow view of segregation also means adopting a narrow view of what the legal system can do about segregation, regardless of how others may define or experience it.

The legal system's narrow approach is not the only reasonable way to address segregation. In fact, researchers and commentators tend to adopt an entirely different approach to the type of segregation deemed important enough to address. They generally assume a much broader view of segregation and its harmful consequences (Levesque, 2015). That view associates the segregation that students experience with discrimination and deems it harmful. For example, it accepts that being educated in places with students mainly of one's race or ethnicity matters. Largely minority schools compared with those that have more White and/or middle-class students have fewer educational resources stemming from differences in teacher quality and experience, parent and student resources, stability of enrollment, advanced instruction, and support for pursuing higher education or specialized employment (Reardon & Owens, 2014). These differences matter because they foster different opportunities that have reverberating effects. Among those effects is the host of social ills associated with missed educational and social opportunities, including economic and other forms of inequality, such as increased child welfare and justice system interventions in their lives. Different opportunities translate into different outcomes—outcomes that can have immeasurable human costs.

The different conceptions of segregation and its effects are said to warrant governmental intervention. In many ways, the broader view of segregation understands its harms as the very ills that led to the Court's historic decision in *Brown*. It suggests the need to address the harms associated with segregation regardless of its causes. It would even go so far as to permit the use of race to determine how one is treated if it can lead to more similar outcomes. Yet, the legal system increasingly moves away from embracing this view of segregation.

The different conceptions of segregation reveal more than a mismatch between what the legal system embraces and reports of people's everyday experiences. The different approaches essentially dictate how society can address inequality. Adopting one approach over the other can lead to rejecting what research has identified as critical to ensuring equality. It even can endorse what research deems as harmful to particular groups in society. If there ever was a time when disagreement over definitions could have such dramatic social consequences, this would be it.

This book explores the source, nature, and implications of disagreements about what constitutes segregation and related phenomena such as desegregation, integration, and discrimination. The source of disagreements is readily identifiable: two Supreme Court cases commonly understood as "*Brown*"—one that overturned the doctrine of "separate but equal" (*Brown I: Brown v. Board of Education*, 1954) and another that provided the remedy for the new conception of equality (*Brown II: Brown v. Board of Education*, 1955). *Brown*, however, remains hotly disputed. The disputes involve what *Brown* really means today. Different views of *Brown*'s mandate emerge because of different legal approaches to understanding its meaning. Those different approaches raise many questions. Among the most important questions are those about the extent to which legal claims reflect empirical reality—what researchers know about segregation and associated phenomena.

Reflecting empirical reality often is not a concern for the legal system. The legal system uses its own set of rules and values to resolve disputes (Levesque, 2014). However, *Brown* provides a different situation. The different interpretations of *Brown* make empirical claims, they raise issues that could be addressed empirically, and researchers have conducted thousands upon thousands of studies addressing these issues. Ignoring what we know is a recipe for failing to provide the justice said to be at the heart of our legal system, regardless of one's view of how to achieve that justice. And, in this instance, privileging one view of *Brown* over another will profoundly affect society. That effect—its harms and benefits—will be differently distributed among different groups depending on the adopted interpretation. The need to ensure fairness in that distribution is all that this area of law is about. That need also is the impetus for this book.

Fundamental Disagreements and Remaining Legal Questions

Relying on *Brown*, all current Supreme Court justices both agree and disagree on important starting points in the government's role in creating and remedying inequality. All agree that government-mandated racial discrimination, without adequate justification, violates the Constitution. That view rests, as articulated in *Brown*, partly on the rationale that government-mandated segregation causes psychological harm and sends the message that Blacks are inferior to Whites. Jurists now accept this proposition as fact. As a result, no one now disputes the default assumption that the legal system should not differentiate among individuals based on their race. That agreement, however, leaves much to disagree about. It leaves open what the legal system can do to counter the lingering effects of its own differential treatment. It especially leaves open what the legal system can permit to address racial disparities that were not directly caused by the legal system itself. In addition, it leaves much of this area of law unsettled.

The now leading interpretation of *Brown* was decided by a highly split Supreme Court decision. That decision, *Parents Involved in Community Schools v. Seattle School District No. 1* (2007), produced no majority opinion and was determined by only one vote. The disagreements stemmed from interpretations of *Brown*'s mandate. No one disputes that *Brown* guides this area of law. But where the law is heading remains to be determined.

Like *Brown, Parents Involved* dealt with efforts to integrate primary and secondary schools. Unlike *Brown*, however, the legal system did not directly create the context—the government was not directly causing the segregation and other ills that the school system sought to remedy. As a result, *Parents Involved* asked the Court to determine how far a school district can go to address segregation that the government did not directly cause. The case asked whether districts can integrate schools that needed integration simply because of where students from different racial groups tended to reside. In legal terms, it asked what the government can do to address de facto situations of racial imbalance.

In considering school districts' use of students' race to determine assignments to schools, the Court dramatically split along two opposing interpretations of *Brown*'s mandate. One group resisted the use of racial classifications to determine access to specific schools and end racial segregation. Another group viewed the consideration of racial classifications as necessary to ensure equal access to specific schools and alleviate racial segregation. Remarkably, the first group of justices embraced *Brown* to halt further integration, whereas the second group also embraced *Brown* to exhort further integration. Despite disagreement and by a thin majority of five justices, the Court rejected the school districts' plans as it found their use of race unjustifiable. As the law now stands, school districts cannot, absent a court mandate to do so, foster the racial integration of their schools and enhance opportunities for minority youth by using race as a factor to determine students' school assignments.

Parents Involved is instructive because it reveals the legal system's two dominant ways of addressing racial disparities in life's chances and experiences: anti-classification and anti-subordination approaches. The anti-classification approach concerns itself with the mere existence of racial classifications. Its general rule is that racial classifications made by the legal system are impermissible because the Constitution's Equal Protection Clause prohibits them and they are inherently harmful. This view rejects classifying people based on race or other protected group characteristics. The anti-classification approach generally bars the use of racial categories even for remedying past societal subjugation. Justice Roberts, writing for the Court, reasoned that the constitutional violation in *Brown* was the legal system's separating children on the basis of race and that achieving full compliance with *Brown* required school districts to achieve a system of determining admission to the public schools on a nonracial basis. He did recognize that other lines of authority permitted the use of race to remedy past practices, but he reasoned that *Brown* had foreclosed the use of those remedies in primary and secondary school contexts. This view led him to conclude that "the way to stop discrimination on the basis of race is to stop discriminating on the basis of race" (*Parents Involved*, 2007, p. 748).

Not all members of the Court adopted Justice Roberts' view; in fact, four did not. These justices maintain that this area of law must recognize and address subjugation. They argue that differential treatment, such as segregation, is problematic because it subjugates disadvantaged groups. This view of differential treatment fashions remedies that combat subjugation. This anti-subordination approach goes beyond identifying racial classifications; it examines why racial imbalances exist and seeks to rebalance them to reduce their harm. To reduce those harms, this approach more readily enlists the legal system to alleviate the subjugation, and it does so even when the legal system itself did not directly cause the subjugation. As Justice Breyer argued in *Parents Involved* (2007, p. 806), "the Constitution cannot plausibly be interpreted to rule out categorically all local efforts to use means that are conscious of the race of individuals" and that "a longstanding and unbroken line of legal authority tells us that the Equal Protection Clause permits local school boards to use race-conscious criteria to achieve positive race-related goals, even when the Constitution does not compel it." In his reasoning, he evoked *Brown* as promising true equality, as permitting racial classification to achieve integration. Unlike the anti-classification approach that seeks to be color-blind, the anti-subordination approach seeks to be color-conscious.

In *Parents Involved*, two justices wrote separately to emphasize diverging approaches to *Brown*. Justice Stevens (*Parents Involved*, 2007, pp. 798–799) dissented to highlight the "cruel irony" in Chief Justice Roberts' reliance on *Brown*. He argued that, by ignoring *Brown*'s focus on the subjugation of an entire race rather than on the need to treat everyone equally on the basis of race, Justice Roberts "rewrites the history of one of this Court's most important decisions" (pp. 798–799). Justice Thomas took an entirely different approach as he supported Justice Roberts. He devoted much of his opinion to linking the dissent's reasoning against a color-blind interpretation of the Constitution to the approaches advocated by the segregationists in *Brown*. By arguing for a legal system that makes no distinctions based on race, he challenged the view that using race for good motives, such as for bringing the races together, justified the use of racial classifications. He found it "the height of arrogance" for members of the Court to assert otherwise (p.778, n. 27).

Despite *Brown*'s undoubted landmark status and its enduring significance, then, jurists and commentators continue to debate what it fully means. As they do so, they argue that their approach remains most faithful to it. Such steadfast reliance on a legal decision may appear odd. But, in this instance, there is nothing odd about it because *Brown* dramatically transformed discrimination law. That transformation means that legal analyses necessarily must return to *Brown* and its view of what the legal system can support when dealing with racial distinctions in particular and inequality in general.

Returning to *Brown* is not an easy task. Challenges arise for many reasons. A key reason involves the manner the Court has since clarified the interpretive standard it uses to protect constitutional rights. The now accepted standard of judicial review systematically evaluates the quality of rights, how they are to be respected, and what constitutes legitimate justifications for infringing on them. This development typically addresses the nature of the right and the government's interest in infringing on it. When it seeks to infringe on important rights, the government has the burden to articulate compelling interests supporting the infringement and the need to infringe in order to further those compelling interests. Because this standard was not explicitly articulated when the Court decided *Brown*, jurists seek to understand how *Brown* fits the standard. Fitting *Brown* into modern standards of analysis becomes challenging because reasonable people can disagree about what *Brown* found, decided, and tried to do.

The disagreement is particularly important because, as is common in law, exceptions to general rules arise. In this instance, the notion that the legal system should not place people into racial classifications for differential treatment has its exceptions. The Court permits the use of classifications, including those based on race, when the government would have a compelling reason to do so, such as to remedy a legally recognizable harm. The most obvious compelling reason that could exist would be that the legal system inappropriately differentiated among groups and caused a harm. All Supreme Court members agree on that compelling reason. However, the Court recognizes other types of harm that the legal system could legitimately address by treating groups differently based on race. As the standard used to address infringements on important rights requires, the intervention to remedy the harm should be as minimal as possible. It should be minimal because using classifications is inherently problematic as it infringes on people's right to be treated equally regardless of race. The intervention is as important to consider as the compelling reason to intervene.

Looking at *Brown* with modern standards to address rights allows justices to disagree. They disagree about the application of every key feature of the standard used to determine the legitimacy of infringing on rights. They disagree about what constitutes discrimination, the harms that come from it, and potential remedies. They even disagree about which standard to apply: Some argue that *Brown* mandated strict standards limiting the use of racial classifications, whereas others find that *Brown* urged flexible approaches.

Many scholars have debated these legal developments since *Brown* and their current resolution. In fact, *Brown* is one of the most cited and analyzed cases in US legal history (Levesque, 2015). This book does not revisit those arguments for determining the legal merits of particular positions. Rather, it evaluates the empirical support for the various legal positions emerging from *Brown* and clarified in *Parents Involved*.

This book examines the empirical foundation of disputes arising from *Brown*'s (1954, p. 495) proclamation "that, in the field of public education, the doctrine of 'separate but equal' has no place." The different views of *Brown*'s mandate mean that this area of law still struggles with key issues that raise empirical matters. How involved must the government be in directly causing segregation before it could be deemed harmful? How harmful must segregation be before the government can embark on desegregating efforts? If desegregation efforts are permissible, what kind of desegregation programs can be instituted? What evidence documents the actual existence of segregation? What actually constitutes segregation: Is it complete or partial disparities in particular schools? If ending segregation involves ending harms, then how must that end be documented? What type of evidence indicates an end to the need for desegregation efforts? What about the benefits of desegregation? Do benefits need to be documented, and what type of evidence would be needed? What about integration efforts that seek to address racial imbalances where there is no segregation? What circumstances make such efforts permissible, and when would the circumstances be sufficiently addressed to no longer warrant the use of remedies? Important empirical issues abound.

Why Empirical Analyses Matter to Resolving Disagreements about Segregation

The government's efforts to address segregation and discrimination may involve empirical issues, but that does not mean that they matter in those efforts. Researchers and jurists routinely argue about the relevance and utility of empirical evidence to judicial decision-making and policy-making. Science and law often are at odds, and the legal system frequently ignores empirical reality or distorts it as often as it embraces and uses it properly. Without doubt, the legal system defines the issues to be addressed and how they will be resolved.

The potential disconnect as well as the potential symbiotic relationship between legal approaches and empirical understandings make empirical research important for several reasons. These reasons are worth emphasizing from the start. Empirical analyses matter because the legal system generally remains receptive to research; the potential relevance of research triggers the need to understand the nature of available research; the Court's reliance on precedence and analogy means that research in one area can influence related domains; empirical research sheds light on the relative importance of the disputed issues; and empirical foundations need a close vetting to guard against their potential misuse. Each of these reasons raises complex matters in efforts to address segregation and its associated phenomena.

The legal system's receptivity and actual use of empirical research makes empirical analyses important to consider. In this regard, *Brown* is known for initiating analyses that evaluate the empirical merit of legal positions. It did so because it references empirical research to support its propositions. Many dispute the relative merit of that research and its relevance to the case's resolution. However, *Brown*'s use of empirical findings is indisputable and, in fact, launched many disciplines that use empirical methods to analyze legal positions (Moran, 2010). Yet another important reason to examine the empirical foundation of legal responses is that the Court's analyses routinely make empirical claims. Not all justices are receptive to empirical findings, but Supreme Court opinions still either rely on them or frame issues that make empirical assumptions. Last, empirical research can inform future legal developments. The use of empirical research now pervades much of policy-making and the administration of law, which means that the research can play a foundational role in shaping disputes and their resolutions.

The empirical merit of the legal system's response to segregation and its modern variants also is important to understand because of the current state of research and its relevance. Racial discrimination, including segregation, actually is one of the most examined topics in the social and behavioral sciences. This volume of research increases even more if we include the tendencies of researchers to examine racial and ethnic differences when they study individuals or groups. That research is important to sort through in light of potentially persuasive legal claims and rationales because those legal aspects dictate the relative significance of empirical evidence. The legal system's different positions on what constitutes rights and harms can result in making irrelevant much empirical research. Those positions also can point to needed research.

Empirical analyses also are important because of the legal system's reliance on precedents and reasoning by analogy. Understanding the empirical foundation of the legal system's response to racial discrimination, particularly segregation, is important because of the manner in which this area of law has influenced many other areas. Vast areas of social life now raise problems of "discrimination," even areas not before seen as raising legal issues or conceptualized as involving differential treatment. In schools, the movement to end discrimination fostered legal and policy changes addressing students' bilingual education, immigration status, disability, gender, socioeconomic status, religion, and sexual orientation (Minow, 2010). These spillover areas may well have made significant progress in ensuring equality of treatment and opportunities, but it remains to be determined whether that progress can continue and result in the type of equality envisioned by ideals of civil rights. Although these spillover movements have their own histories, some of which are quite brief, the lessons from *Brown* can be instructive. *Brown*, and what ensued from it, remains the paradigmatic case for addressing discrimination and differential treatment.

Empirical analyses also matter because racial and ethnic imbalances figure prominently in our society. Researchers reveal that for the past several years, schools have been segregated more racially than they were at the height of the desegregation effort, and the segregation continues to increase (Clotfelter, 2001, 2004). More than 70 percent of all African American and Latino students in the United States attend largely minority schools (Frankenberg, Lee, & Orfield, 2003). Other researchers also demonstrate that, when court oversight of desegregation efforts ends, segregation typically returns (Lutz, 2011; Reardon, Grwal, Kalogrides, & Greenberg, 2012). Yet other researchers show how even the high figures indicating a lack of integration do not reflect the extent of segregation based on race. They reveal that bringing youth of different ethnicities to the same institution need not result in its integration. This lack of integration occurs because students informally tend to segregate themselves; students tend to associate with peers of their own ethnicity, especially when in ethnically diverse schools (Levesque, 2014). Lack of integration also occurs because some school programs and policies lead to the internal segregation of schools, as illustrated by research on the implementation of academic tracks, ability grouping, special education and alternative schooling, and high-stakes testing (Walsemann & Bell, 2010). Thus, despite increasing efforts to integrate schools and limit the segregation of students on the basis of noticeable markers, schools may stymie integration efforts if minority and majority students simply resegregate themselves or are placed in situations that foster resegregation.

The existence of racial and ethnic imbalances in society is important because they link to harm. Much research supports claims of the multiple negative outcomes associated with discrimination and differential treatment (Kim, Losen, & Hewitt, 2010; Walsemann & Bell, 2010). The legal system has long recognized the pernicious effects of that ill treatment. In fact, *Brown* itself noted the psychological damage of differential treatment as it famously noted that separation "generates a feeling of inferiority" that affects Black students' "hearts and minds" (*Brown*, 1954, p. 494). It understood segregation as facilitating status diminution in that separation "denotes the inferiority of the negro group" (p. 494). It further reasoned that segregation excludes Blacks from educational and other social opportunities afforded only to White students when it found that education is the "very foundation of good citizenship" and thus "must be made available to all on equal terms" (p. 493). Without doubt, different racial circumstances and opportunities have important effects on individual as well as societal development.

Last, empirical understandings matter because of their potential misuse. Important grounds for cautiously relying on empirical findings can be found both in the nature of empirical evidence and in the legal system's use of it. In terms of the nature of empirical evidence, empirical research clearly has a checkered past. Before *Brown*, for example, scientific theories and analyses of race aligned perfectly well with constitutional theories to support many forms of subordination, including subordination relating to what have become the protected classifications of ethnicity, religion, gender, or nationality. Dominant ideologies of social inequality pervaded scientific theories and judicial interpretations. Although modern empirical approaches may guard against spurious science, those very approaches themselves urge caution.

In terms of the use of empirical evidence by the legal system, several examples reveal the potential misuse of empirical findings. Notably, reliance on the adversarial system to reach legal decisions may not be conducive to the appropriate use of empirical findings. This is so because, for example, specific legal issues in controversy limit decision makers' use of evidence, and the dominant way that courts receive empirical evidence—through amicus briefs—necessarily blends science translation and advocacy. In essence, the legal system muddies the type of evidence brought to a court's attention, and empirical evidence itself is not immune from furthering problematic facts. The same impulses emerge in legislative processes, which by their very nature are "political"—the process results in responding to some facts and not to others. The potential misuse justifiably gives pause to anyone championing and analyzing empirical foundations used to resolve legal disputes.

Without doubt, then, empirical examinations matter. They can inform legal decisions that go to the heart of civil society. They can provide a sense of the issues' importance. In doing so, they permit evaluations of the relative merit of different positions and how they can be resolved. In essence, they may not determine the legal merit of particular rules or outcomes, but they can reveal their relative effectiveness. What we know about the harms associated with segregation makes pressing a close analysis of the empirical realities that underlie legal disputes about it. The analysis is even more pressing given that the current leading case, *Parents Involved*, leaves this area of law unsettled as members of the Court address the merit of different ways to conceptualize and address racial and ethnic differences in opportunities.

The Chapters Ahead

Chapter 2 examines the general parameters of how the legal system addresses claims alleging violations of rights, such as those involving differential treatment based on race. The analysis demonstrates when discrimination exists in law and, equally important, shows what is needed to envision ways to reach societal interests relating to equal opportunities and equal treatment. The chapter ends by noting how these legal developments influence the potential relevance and utility of empirical evidence.

Chapter 3 details how the legal system applies the legal developments to racial classifications. That analysis centers on the extent to which the government retains a compelling interest to assert a need for differential treatment and the extent to which the government's actions reach the intended goals of furthering those compelling interests. To do so, the analysis proceeds in two directions. The first line of analysis examines reasons identified by the legal system to treat people differently on the basis of race, such as the need to remedy past discrimination, address governmental discrimination, enhance diversity, remedy societal discrimination, and secure democratic ideals. The second line of analysis involves reasons identified for not treating people differently based on their racial status, such as the need to avoid stigma, group hostility, the loss of government benefits, and the usurpation of local powers. Presenting these analyses reveals how the legal system raises questions that readily lend themselves to empirical formulations. The chapter ends by presenting some of the key challenges raised by empirical evaluations of legal rationales, which sets the stage for the remainder of the book.

Chapter 4 evaluates empirical evidence addressing the two fundamental approaches to segregation and diversity: anti-classification (resisting differential treatment) and anti-subordination (permitting differential treatment). The anti-classification approach, which seeks to reject legal classifications based on race, rejects desegregation efforts unless the legal system was directly involved in creating the classification that segregated. That is, desegregation involves undoing segregation that the government created, unlike integration, which involves bringing different racial groups together regardless of the reason they originally were separated. Available empirical evidence actually supports the need to limit desegregation efforts. In fact, research does not appear to even support the legal rationales for engaging in desegregation to remedy segregation imposed by the government. This is a striking conclusion given social scientists' pervasive and heated opposition to the anti-classification approach. The little empirical support for desegregation's achieving the goals of its articulated rationales appears due to developments in law, lagging social science efforts to address those developments, and social scientists' apparent misunderstanding of legal issues. The lack of support also derives from the reality that anti-classification approaches do not allow for engaging in new research to address its concerns. However, the available evidence remains far from a ringing endorsement of anti-classification principles—some forms of segregation have benefits, and desegregation efforts can fail to achieve goals. Still, the anti-classification approach rightly holds that the government's use of race should generate considerable scrutiny.

Chapter 4's analysis of the anti-subordination approach also results in a striking conclusion given that researchers pervasively support the approach while the results of relevant empirical research remain tentative. The anti-subordination approach would allow integration efforts, even when the legal system did not explicitly segregate. To permit integration, the legal system requires those seeking to use legal classifications based on race to demonstrate that they address appropriate compelling governmental interests. This leads to several empirical analyses of multiple compelling governmental interests supporting efforts to embark on integration efforts (rather than desegregation). Again, the nature of the legal requirements makes obtaining empirical support considerably challenging. Despite much research in this area, little of it actually supports the needs articulated by the legal system. Although current findings do reveal some support for anti-subordination impulses, the approach does not have much empirical justification. Integration to increase diversity at primary and secondary school levels may not increase diverse viewpoints, nor does it necessarily reduce racial isolation and the harms associated with it. Integration generally increases academic success, but important variations exit. Findings on civic participation and occupational outcomes remain more equivocal. The upshot is that researchers, legal decision-makers, and even society as a whole may have strong attachments to anti-subordination impulses, but those do not match well with what the legal system requires to support them. Importantly, the conclusion is not that anti-subordination efforts are ineffective; the point is that, as framed by what the legal system deems relevant, the approach lacks empirical merit.

Chapter 5 analyzes research relating to the necessity of remedial approaches as well as potential alternatives. These constitute critical analyses due to the manner in which the Supreme Court addresses group classifications relating to race. Recall that even if the legal system finds that the government inappropriately segregated youth or that it has compelling reasons to integrate schools, it is still important to address how the government can implement remedies. To do so, the government must show that the remedy is necessary and that no reasonably effective alternative exists. This analysis reveals scant empirical evidence that addresses the law's direct needs. Notably, it is not clear that integration efforts that use racial classifications are necessary to address the ills described by the legal system. In addition, it is not clear that alternatives, such as using economic status to shape school districts, increase integration in ways that reduce the harms associated with discrimination. In the end, the conclusion is not that these approaches could not receive empirical support; it is just that researchers simply have not engaged in the type of research needed to address key legal claims.

Chapter 6 concludes the analysis. The overall conclusion that emerges is that empirical findings may play a role in shaping legal responses, but the bulk of current research increasingly becomes irrelevant. This is a striking conclusion given the abundance of studies addressing the nature and effects of racial disparities and what to do about them. An examination of current research actually reveals unexpected findings that do not support policy propositions made by researchers. This is not to say that researchers misrepresent their findings; it is to say that their findings typically lack legal relevance. The legal system and researchers appear to be moving in opposite directions in what they identify as problematic and what to do about it. This concluding chapter sorts through the lessons learned about the legal system's evaluation of empirical research. It highlights the problematic nature of legal approaches, which now focus on remaining neutral/color-blind with regard to racial disparities. It then details how the legal system can better benefit from research that addresses racial and ethnic disparities.

The six chapters of this volume develop one message: The legal system now has clarified the principles supporting laws that relate to segregation, desegregation, integration, and discrimination. It began with a strong, unanimous stand in *Brown* and culminated with strong disagreements in *Parents Involved*. The disagreements in *Parents Involved* clearly articulated how the Court will resolve disputes. By re-examining *Brown* and legal developments since then, the Court has clarified the types of arguments that will matter and its relative openness to empirical analysis. Rather than finding a settled area of law, we find a dynamic one that calls for close analyses of different positions. Those analyses reveal unexpected conclusions that ask for different legal and empirical work to address pervasive mismatches among legal, empirical, and societal needs.

The message is not just an "academic" one. The law does not square with people's experiences. The legal system's effectiveness in addressing school segregation reveals, from a practical perspective, that segregation persists and even surpasses levels before the civil rights movement. Yet, the legal system continues as though segregation is a thing of the past. Even more bizarre, the legal system compels itself to ignore the well-documented negative effects of racial and ethnic disparities in schooling. To exacerbate matters, legal analysts increasingly interpret the law as a system that operates in a different world than the one documented by researchers who describe disparities and what could be done about them. For their part, researchers continue to document experiences without considering the legal system's basic concerns. These circumstances spur the need for understanding the source of these gaps, evaluating their empirical and legal foundation, explaining why they persist, and revealing what can be done about them.

2

Determining the Legitimacy of Laws That Use Racial/Ethnic Classifications

The Law's Concern for the Same or Different Treatment

Under the US Constitution, the government must ensure that individuals receive the equal protection of laws. This mandate, however, becomes challenging in that equal protection may be different depending on the involved individuals and circumstances. Depending on the relevance of group differences particular to different circumstances, the equal protection mandate may not require the same treatment. The Constitution accommodates for this principle to the extent that some groups of people are inherently different and thus can be treated differently. The use of this principle rests on the recognition that it would be unjust for the law to treat different (or differently situated) people as though they were the same or in identical circumstances. This possibility raises this area of law's fundamental dilemma: Treating people differently emphasizes difference and likely can cause harm, whereas treating all individuals alike can be insensitive to difference and also can cause harm. This dilemma is important to understand because it remains at the center of segregation law—at the center of the legal system's classifying individuals to treat them differently through segregation, desegregation, or integration efforts.

Permitting or prohibiting differential treatment, and the risks inherent in either approach, raises two important questions. First, what constitutes difference and permissible differential treatment? Second, who legitimately can be involved in creating or ignoring a classification between groups leading to differential treatment? The legal system addresses these questions in complex ways.

Determining the legitimacy of the legal system's approach to identifying and achieving equality involves subjecting the government's group-based classifications to various levels of scrutiny. The application of these levels of scrutiny ultimately determines whether and how the legal system must treat members of a particular group the same as members of other groups. That determination centers on the extent to which the government retains a compelling interest in asserting a need for differential treatment, with some compelling interests deemed more compelling than others, and the extent to which the government's actions reach the intended goals of furthering compelling interests (if those goals indeed are deemed compelling enough to pursue). This type of review typically is challenging to apply and challenging to understand. But knowing the parameters of these challenges, particularly as they relate to the legal system's approach to diversity, is necessary for understanding the relative relevance of empirical research and the extent to which empirical work meets the legal system's needs.

Foundational Points of Departure

Understanding complexities in this area of law requires understanding four foundational points of departure. The first point relates to the actions that fall within the Constitution's equal protection mandate. The mandate applies to claims against all federal, state, and local governments. The language of the Fourteenth Amendment's Equal Protection Clause mandates that "no state shall . . . deny to any person within its jurisdiction the equal protection of the laws" and thus actually applies only to state and local governments within them. However, through a process of "reverse incorporation," the Supreme Court has applied the limitation to the federal government. The Court did so in *Bolling v. Sharpe* (1954), a landmark civil rights case unanimously decided the same day as *Brown v. Board of Education* (1954), which held school segregation in the District of Columbia's public schools unconstitutional under the Due Process Clause of the Fifth Amendment by inferring from that amendment an equal protection component applicable to the federal government.

In addition to applying to all levels of government, the equal protection mandate applies to both legislative and executive actions. Those governmental actions include both substantive and procedural law, with substantive laws referring to the obligations and rights of people and legal entities and procedural laws referring to the steps and procedures involved in enforcing civil and criminal laws. Equally important, if a court engages in creating rules (i.e., in creating what is known as common law), those rules also are subject to equal protection requirements. Indeed, the judiciary itself must follow equal protection mandates. At its core, then, the mandate offering equal protection of laws limits all governmental actions. This may seem like an obvious point. However, the focus on governmental actions becomes important when dealing with legal issues relating to inequality. The requirement severely circumscribes what counts as inequality and what does not; it also dictates what legal systems can do to address the problematic and harmful treatment of some individuals. For better or for worse, equal protection mandates fundamentally involve the government's own actions.

The second foundational point is that the Equal Protection Clause does not state who determines the grounds for distinction—who determines whether inequality exists and the government's appropriate response. This lack of specificity raises the fundamental political question of which branch of government can claim the power to permit and justify different kinds of unequal treatment. As a result, tensions exist between the judicial and other branches of government. These tensions involve a continuum between judicial activism and judicial deference in efforts to resolve the following fundamental question: How and to what extent should judges arrive at answers to disputes that turn on value judgments, without substituting themselves for the legislative/executive branches or abdicating their responsibility to protect against abuses by the majority? This question results in the tension between whether legislatures (and executive branches) can lay a superior claim to legitimacy in making these value judgments, which would limit the judiciary's scrutiny to the question of whether the political process has been undermined, or whether the judiciary should decide whether the challenged actions conflict with clear and entrenched principles.

Our system of government already has decided which branch of government can claim the power over others. Courts retain the power to distinguish and umpire between legal and illegal differentiation. However, the tension remains and often emerges in judicial decisions. Courts consider and respect their role in a multibranch system of government that limits their role. That is, courts, as well as other branches of government, must address thorny allegations of unequal treatment in ways that do not inappropriately usurp the power of communities to determine what is best for themselves.

The third foundational point relates to the judiciary's implementation of its powers, which is this: The nature of the approach that courts take to scrutinize governmental actions that are challenged on equal protection grounds. In this regard, the US Supreme Court has developed an elaborate system of differing levels of scrutiny for determining the extent to which the government can justify different kinds of differential treatment. The analytical schemes used to assess the constitutionality of governmental actions are important to consider given that they inevitably determine the outcome of disputes, including whether the law can treat a group of individuals differently from those in other groups and, if so, what constitutes a legally recognizable group of individuals that the law can treat differently. The schemes also are of significance for the simple reason that they determine what matters for determining difference that would then relate to the recognition of a group and what aspects of difference matter enough to enlist equal protection of laws mandates. Thus, the grounds for recognizing a group and who could count as part of it, and then when that recognition matters, all are the subject of important rules that must be considered carefully when evaluating whether the legal system acts legitimately in its differential (or even identical) treatment of individuals.

The fourth foundational point relates to the significance of the government's actually making classifications. This area of law concerns itself with the government's classification of individuals. If the government enacts laws and policies that affect individuals from particular racial/ethnic groups differently but the differential effect is not due to the government's direct use of a racial/ethnic classification, then the government's actions avoid judicial review. Absent allegations that illicit motives drove the actions leading to the disparities, the Court views the difference in effects as a necessary by-product of the government's need to make decisions bound to differentially affect different groups. For example, the government can differentially treat people based on classifications that do not received heightened constitutional protection, such as socioeconomic status. Those actions may influence different racial/ethnic groups differently and may be permissible when the classification is not based on prohibited group status. The significance of this starting point is that the government can avoid scrutiny—that the major work of reviewing courts centers on whether the government could make an explicit classification based on racial/ethnic status.

Judicial Review's Focus on Suspect Classifications

When determining the legitimacy of governmental actions under the Equal Protection Clause, the Supreme Court's analysis necessarily depends on the nature of the legal challenge, which results in a varying amount of deference to the governmental actors who have enacted laws and policies and those who implement them. That variation in deference ranges widely. Under one extreme, challenged laws, policies, and actions can survive judicial scrutiny due to the courts' granting the government a large amount of discretion, whereas under the other extreme, the governments' actions can be overturned due to courts' need to conduct searching and demanding reviews. To that end, the Court has developed standards to assess the constitutionality of governmental actions that raise constitutional equal protection issues. These standards actually are easy to describe and understand. As with many areas of law, however, their application remains less than obvious because members of a court do not always agree on which standard to apply and, when they do agree, their application of the law to particular cases still can lead to different outcomes. It is this diversity that leads us to highlight the nature of these analytical standards and their significance.

The Court has fashioned what has become known as suspect classification jurisprudence to elaborate on the guarantee of equal protection. The Court used the term *suspect* to describe the government's actions toward groups, not the relevant groups themselves. The more suspect the classification, the more scrutiny it receives from the judiciary. Although disputes continue regarding efforts to understand how the Court truly approaches this scrutiny and takes its own analytical schemes seriously, courts and commentators typically identify three forms of review (rational basis review, intermediate scrutiny, and strict scrutiny) that a reviewing court could use depending on the individual or group affected by the government's actions and the nature of the involved rights.

The three levels of review are analytically important for determining the outcomes of cases in that they also refer to the standard to which the government will be held. In that regard, the Court holds the government to a higher standard (meaning that it more readily limits the government) when the Court deems more important the rights that would be infringed. The rights that gain the most protection typically are those deemed as fundamental, which in turn typically means that the Constitution has enumerated them as in need of protection. That higher standard of protection essentially means that the government must claim greater cause if it wishes to infringe on rights explicitly recognized as more important, and the government must limit its infringement to those most necessary to achieve the state's compelling interests. The more searching judicial inquiry into classifications permits courts to distinguish between benign classifications and those motivated by illegitimate notions of inferiority and discriminatory animus.

Determining whether a policy or law meets the guarantee of equal protection, then, largely depends on the standard of review that a court applies. As a result, properly understanding what a court must do in cases that challenge laws on equal protection grounds must begin with a close consideration of the standards of judicial review and their application to a variety of classifications.

Strict Scrutiny Review

The concept of strict scrutiny relates to the history of the Fourteenth Amendment, and the developments in the manner the Court has interpreted how it will implement the Amendment's mandate that "no state . . . deny to any person within its jurisdiction the equal protection of the laws." Notably, the Constitution's equal protection of laws mandate was long considered intended purely to protect the slaves freed after the American Civil War. It was adopted on July 9, 1868, as one of three Reconstruction Amendments adopted after the Civil War to "reconstruct" the American South and transform the United States into a nation that had abolished slavery and extended liberties to slaves (actually, at that point in history, to male slaves). As a result, courts initially treated the Amendment as calling only for scrutiny of laws that classified individuals according to race (*Slaughter-House Cases*, 1873; *Strauder v. West Virginia*, 1880).

The narrow focus on race changed in the late 1930s with the now famous *United States v. Carolene Products Company* (1938). That case dealt with cow milk. Specifically, *Carolene Products* addressed the legitimacy of a federal law that prohibited filled milk (skimmed milk compounded with any fat or oil other than milk fat so as to resemble milk or cream) from being shipped in interstate commerce. The Court found that the law, as part of the regulation of commerce, was "presumptively constitutional" due to its resting on a legislative judgment. The Court reasoned that the judiciary lacked authority to overrule the law because it was neither arbitrary nor irrational in light of the substantial public health evidence.

The Court, however, did not stop there. The Court offered Footnote 4, a note deemed the most famous footnote in Constitutional law, that proposed a new level of review for certain other types of cases. The Court suggested that other types of cases should apply a more exacting standard of judicial review, specifically when legislation takes aim at "discrete and insular minorities" who lack the normal protections of the political process (*Id.*, p. 152). Such cases, the Court noted, provided an exception to the presumption of constitutionality and required a heightened standard of judicial review.

Caroline Products' footnote introduced the need to apply "strict scrutiny" when the government infringed on a fundamental right or distinguished individuals on a basis that singled out a discrete and insular minority and thus engaged in creating a "suspect classification." Under this analytical scheme, a measure would satisfy strict scrutiny if it was tailored narrowly to achieve a compelling governmental interest. Any other classification would satisfy the equal protection mandate as long as the distinction bore a rational relationship to a legitimate governmental objective. In essence, the Court reasoned that the Equal Protection Clause protected against disparate treatment on illegitimate, irrational, or purely arbitrary grounds, and the Court adopted a presumption that distinctions inimical to an identified minority group, or that restricted fundamental liberties, denied that protection.

The Supreme Court first applied the higher level of scrutiny in *Korematsu v. United States* (1944). That case was not only the first time that the Court applied its strict scrutiny analysis but also the first time that the Court used the approach to support the government's classification that permitted racial discrimination. *Korematsu* is the landmark case that upheld the constitutionality of Executive Order 9066, which authorized the relocation of Japanese Americans into internment camps during World War II. That mass incarceration occurred without charges, notice, trial, or due process and without any evidence of espionage and sabotage by persons of Japanese ancestry. The order was challenged by Korematsu, an American citizen of Japanese descent convicted of remaining in a military area contrary to the executive order.

The Court held that the need to protect against espionage outweighed Korematsu's individual rights as well as those of Americans of Japanese descent. The majority ruled in favor of the administration on the grounds of the need to defer to Congress and the military during times of national emergencies. The Court was well aware that it was permitting distinctions based on race, as two dissenting opinions had pointed to the significance of race, with one opinion outrightly accusing the majority of racism. Despite concerns about racism and inappropriate discrimination, the Court found the government's interests compelling and appropriately implemented.

Although the order was not clearly rational, particularly as applied in some contexts, the Court deemed it appropriate. For example, the order declared that Korematsu could not be in a military area but also decreed that he may not be outside an assembly center. For Korematsu, the only way he could arrive at an assembly center would be to pass through the military area. Faced with conflicting orders, Korematsu made the understandable choice of doing nothing. That lack of clarity did not stop the Court from supporting it. Although criticized, *Korematsu* still stands for upholding the indefinite detention of citizens without due process based on ancestry. The case remains a clear example of the extent to which the Court will defer to other branches of government when they have compelling interests.

In addition to clarifying the important role of the government's compelling state interests, legal developments also clarified the significance of the classifications themselves. By the 1970s, the "discrete and insular minority" underpinning of strict scrutiny analyses ceased to control whether the Court would view a classification as "suspect." The Court began to view racial distinctions as intrinsically problematic for reasons beyond political participation. Rather than limit itself to concerns that some groups lacked protections in political processes, the Court focused on the classifications themselves. As a result, for example, classifications making racial distinctions that burdened Whites, such as affirmative action, also were treated as suspect (*Regents of the University of California v. Bakke*, 1978).

This move emerged from a series of important cases in which the Court reaffirmed the need for reviewing courts to use strict scrutiny for all racial classifications. They needed to do so regardless of whether the policies subordinate minorities, remedy past discrimination, or promote the inclusion of minorities in civic life. The Court deemed racial classifications as in need of strict scrutiny regardless of the race of those burdened or benefitted (*Adarand Constructors, Inc. v. Peña*, 1995; *City of Richmond v. J. A. Croson Co.*, 1989). This would become even more obvious as the most recent cases would focus on the classification itself (see *Parents Involved in Community Schools v. Seattle School District No. 1*, 2007). This approach would be reinforced by cases that did not focus on minority status at all, such as, most notably, classifications based on national origin that would be subjected to strict scrutiny and deemed as highly suspect without reference to minority status (*Graham v. Richardson*, 1971). Similarly, even classifications relating to religion would result in strict scrutiny analyses, although the rationale for doing so also would be linked to the need to protect important rights on the grounds that such classifications may invade the fundamental right to the free exercise of religion (*Employment Division v. Smith*, 1990). The past few decades, then, witnessed a spread in the classifications that would warrant the Court's close scrutiny.

As it has developed to include more classifications worthy of enhanced analysis, strict scrutiny review still has remained the highest standard that the Court will use to consider the legitimacy of a government's actions. Currently, a court focuses on both substantive and procedural grounds in its analysis of challenges to governmental actions that classify individuals according to their group status. Substantively, the standard requires that the government be pursuing a compelling objective that relates closely to its legal mandates. Procedurally, the standard requires that the challenged mandate pursues that objective through the least rights-infringing approach among reasonably available means.

These two elements mean that classifications challenged on the grounds that they infringe on the right to be treated equally must further a compelling government interest and must be necessary to the extent that it is narrowly tailored to achieve that end that other reasonable means would not achieve. At their core, these analyses necessarily place the judicial system as the stringent arbiter of governmental mandates, one that severely limits the government because of the great protection granted to individuals' right not to be treated differently by being placed in inappropriate classifications. Given that this analytical scheme bestows considerable power on the courts, and its legitimacy must be guarded closely given the tensions noted previously, the application of strict scrutiny necessarily still remains limited to classifications that the legal system views as inherently suspect and worthy of the highest protection, and thus enumerated in the Constitution: race, national origin, and religion.

Strict scrutiny may offer the highest protection against unequal treatment, as it has been famously called "strict in theory" and "fatal in fact" (Gunther, 1972, p. 8), but it does not inevitably mean that classifications will run afoul of the Constitution. The companion affirmative action cases of *Grutter v. Bollinger* (2003) and *Gratz v. Bollinger* (2003) illustrate well, for example, how the rationales and nature of the classification matter. *Grutter* involved the University of Michigan Law School's admissions policy, whereas *Gratz* involved the same university's policies relating to undergraduate admissions. Both policies used race as a factor in admissions, and they did so to improve diversity for educational purposes. However, the Court accepted one policy and rejected the other.

The Court's different responses to the Michigan cases reveal the importance of the rationale for differently treating individuals based on their racial status. The Supreme Court accepted the diversity rationale to support the use of racial classifications but rejected the notion that the state had a compelling interest in redressing the racial imbalances created by centuries of slavery and second-class citizenship. As a result, the only way that the admissions policy could be deemed legitimate was if it was appropriately serving the government's interest in educational diversity. The admissions policies were quite different, partly because they had different goals. *Gratz*'s policy used a point system that gave African American applicants additional points because of their race. *Grutter*'s policy adopted a more nuanced and flexible approach as it also took race into account but did so only as one of several factors not given a numerical value.

The Court's focus on procedural aspects reveals again the importance of the classification. Having accepted the rationale that the government had a compelling interest in ensuring diversity, the Court required the admissions policies to be tailored narrowly to that compelling interest. That requirement means that the classification must achieve its objectives relating to the compelling interest and that it imposes no more adverse effects than necessary to reach those objectives. As a result, *Grutter*'s flexibility in its policy saved it from being overturned. The flexibility permitted the admissions committees to account for factors other than race, which might contribute to diversity, and it also permitted the committee to discount race in a case in which it might not actually make the student body more diverse. Unlike *Grutter*'s policy, the one in *Gratz* failed on the grounds that it was possible for the boost in points to result in a student's admission when it did not improve the diversity of the class; it also failed because, in some other instances, the boost in points could result in rejecting a White student who could bring diversity to the school. The *Grutter* and *Gratz* cases confirm that rationales and responses to classifications are important because they determine the appropriateness of classifications.

By supporting different results for classifications based on similar and highly protected classifications (race), *Grutter* and *Gratz* provide important lessons. They provide the lesson that the possibility of over-breadth (protecting those who do not need protection) or under-inclusiveness (not protecting those who do need protection) is fatal under strict scrutiny and that the classification will survive if the possibility could be avoided. The cases also reveal that measures with no more discriminatory impact than necessary to accomplish the legitimate objective will survive strict scrutiny regardless of the extent of that impact. Last, the cases demonstrate that courts focus on formal possibilities and actually permit actions that allow (but do not require) discretion and thus also permit actual discrimination by condoning the flexibility. It is quite remarkable that the Court approves of the program that relies on discretion in the use of race while rejecting one that would remove the discretion, as it would seem that discretion contributes to discrimination. This approval highlights the Court's hesitance to require the government to treat individuals differently based on a racial classification and an effort to compromise by permitting the use of classifications to achieve compelling governmental interests.

That strict scrutiny analyses still permit the use of classifications based on race was reinforced recently in two cases involving affirmative action programs at the University of Texas. In the wake of *Grutter* and *Gratz*, the university evaluated its admissions policies and found them wanting in terms of providing the educational benefits of a diverse student body to all of its students. It then enacted a program that, in part, considered a student's race. In 2013, the Court, in *Fisher v. University of Texas at Austin* (*Fisher I*), rejected an appellate court's decision supporting the university on the grounds that the court had applied an overly deferential, "good faith" standard in evaluating the university's policy and supporting evidence allowing for the use of racial classifications. In doing so, the Supreme Court essentially requested that the lower court conduct a more searching determination, one traditionally aligned with strict scrutiny.

Given the Court's apparent focus on the need to adhere to strict scrutiny, many expected the Court to eventually strike down the policy. However, that was not to be. Upon reconsideration, the appellate court simply affirmed its earlier judgment without further remanding the case to the district court; the court failed to do what typically would have been expected if it wanted to bolster its evidentiary analysis. The Supreme Court then accepted an appeal of that case and affirmed in *Fisher v. University of Texas at Austin* (2016) (*Fisher II*). The Supreme Court examined the evidence that had been available to it the first time and found that the university had offered reasoned, principled explanations for its decisions, had studied and deliberated for months before enacting its policy, had supported its conclusion by significant and anecdotal evidence, and had used the only available workable means. In so ruling, the Supreme Court ultimately did defer to the school's authority, but it did so in a manner that affirmed the need for the government (here, the University of Texas) to provide significant evidence and principled explanations. Although the justices were split in terms of the evidentiary support, the case nevertheless stands for flexibility in applying strict scrutiny, at least for post-secondary admissions policies.

This area of law also highlights the important point that the state's role in dealing with classifications considerably matters. For example and quite famously, in *Brown v. Board of Education* (1954), the Supreme Court concluded that the use of racial classifications to segregate students violated the Equal Protection Clause. However, in *Green v. County School Board of New Kent County* (1968), the Court required public schools to use racial classifications to eliminate the vestiges of its prior discriminatory conduct. The Court rejected the argument that nonracial means could be instituted to remedy the harm of de jure—government created—segregation. Thus, the Supreme Court cases that directly have addressed the use of racial classifications by public schools have found their use to further segregation unconstitutional, but it also has found their use legitimate to remedy equal protection violations. The government's use of racial classifications, such as thorough policies relating to public schools, does not amount to a per se equal protection violation. These cases also show that if it uses a racial distinction, even for a benign (affirmative) purpose, the law must satisfy the same strict test of discrimination in favor of a member of a protected classification as opposed to discrimination against one. The government cannot avoid close scrutiny when it makes classifications based on race.

Rational Basis Review

The rational basis level of review, sometimes called the "rational basis test," denotes the default level of scrutiny. This analytical approach requires courts to engage in only a minimal level of scrutiny to determine the legitimacy of the challenged governmental action. The approach deems a more searching scrutiny unnecessary on the presumption that the government acted permissibly simply because the classification does not warrant much protection. This is even the case, for example, when a challenged legislative mandate does not even have adequate source materials to help a court determine the grounds for the legislative action. In instances that require only a rational review of a governmental action, a court will reject a statutory classification only when no conceivable grounds can justify the classification. In a real sense, as long as the government's actions rationally relate to a legitimate governmental interest, the court defers to the government and supports its actions. The Court's holding the government to such a low standard exemplifies why the standard is labeled only a "review," not anything close to "scrutiny."

The deference to the government is so strong that a reviewing court can even develop its rationales for supporting the government's actions when the government itself failed to articulate appropriate ones. This stance essentially means that a reviewing court can go out of its way to support the government as offering an acceptable governmental interest that need not be one that actually motivated the government to act. Under this standard of review, the court generally will uphold the governmental action so long as the court evaluates the relevant parties' advanced interest as conceivable, even those conceived after the policy's enactment. As a result, the "legitimate interest" need not be the government's actual interest. As long as a court can hypothesize a "legitimate" interest served by the challenged action, the action will withstand the rational basis review. This is of significance in that, for example, a statute can be enacted on the basis of impermissible grounds but, when the case is challenged, rational arguments could be made to support the statute and, as a result, the statute would pass constitutional muster.

Although a reviewing court can grant the government considerable flexibility, the court must find that the government has, at the very least, acted rationally. The court does not sustain governmental actions deemed irrational. Still, the standard is easy to meet. It does not require very much on the government's part to enact and justify a mandate that has the semblance of rationality.

Although the rational basis level of review would seem straightforward, it has not avoided controversy. The approach defers to the government and simply asks that its actions be a reasonable means to an end that the government can pursue legitimately. Thus, the action must relate to a legitimate government interest, which essentially means that the government cannot act arbitrarily. This type of review does make considerable sense when the government is not dealing with highly protected interests. The approach makes sense because the government cannot target a group to suffer an important harm that another group arbitrarily avoids. The approach ensures that the government has freedom to act and that it will act legitimately. Conversely, the nature of the review taken by a rational basis approach has been viewed as excessively deferential, and it has been criticized as an inappropriate abdication of judicial responsibility. This criticism often surfaces because a court will not engage in second-guessing a governmental action. Importantly, this minimal level of review does not require that the government action be wise or reach a high level of scientific accuracy. As former Justice John Paul Stevens attributed to Justice Thurgood Marshall, "The Constitution does not prohibit legislatures from enacting stupid laws" (*New York State Board of Elections v. Lopez Torres*, 2008, p. 209), and numerous Supreme Court opinions uphold mandates that the justices themselves do not view as wise. Yet, some justices do not hesitate to find unwise mandates impermissible, which fuels controversy regarding the Court's fidelity to its own standards. A stupid law can be rational to one person but irrational to another.

Despite controversies and realities when put into practice, the application of the rational basis type of inquiry results in having the vast majority of cases applying this level of review avoid serious scrutiny, if any. The "legitimate governmental objective" prong of the test simply requires that the government articulate an interest acceptable as legitimate to a reviewing court. Generally, courts need not ask whether this appears to be the true objective of the measure. Provided that what the government claims it seeks to accomplish does not strike the court as illegitimate, the rational relationship prong of the test demands only the existence of "any reasonably conceivable state of facts that could provide a rational basis for the classification" (*FCC v. Beach Communications*, 1993, p. 313).

The approach also tips the balance in favor of the government in the way that it burdens those challenging the governmental actions and the high burden they must meet. In supporting its claims of pursuing legitimate governmental objectives, the government need not produce any actual evidence supporting its rationales. This is unlike the strict scrutiny approach that requires the government to demonstrate, for example, not only that it has a compelling interest but also that it considered other means of furthering those interests. Rather, a claimant challenging the government bears the burden of proving the absence of such facts—that the government's actions are not reasonable. In this regard, courts only need to be convinced of a plausible explanation that connects the distinction among groups and the government's objectives. Further unlike the strict scrutiny level of inquiry, the rational basis of review entails no concern for over-breadth and under-inclusiveness. These rules mean that those challenging classifications under the Equal Protection Clause likely will lose their claims unless they can convince a court to apply a heightened level of scrutiny; if they cannot do so, their claims will rest on the basic principle of due process that laws must not be irrational.

Although the rational basis review may be criticized for not having much bite and for permitting the judiciary's abdication of its duties, the Court's jurisprudence does provide instances pointing to a rigorous application of the rational basis test. The Court most notably used a heightened form of rational basis review in *Plyler v. Doe* (1982), a case involving a challenge to a Texas law that denied a public education to the children of illegal aliens. In determining the rationality of the statute, the Court took into account its costs to the nation, namely denying a class of children the means to absorb the values and skills on which social order rests. The Court also considered costs to the children in the form of the inestimable toll that a lack of education would have on their social, economic, intellectual, and psychological well-being, as well as the obstacle a lack of education poses to advancement on the basis of individual merit. Framed in this manner, the Court increased the government's burden to demonstrate the rationality of its policies; it put the government's justifications to the test of whether it would achieve its broader goals.

The *Plyler* Court rejected the government's justifications. The Court found insufficient the state's interest in preserving the state's limited resources for the education of its lawful residents, protecting itself in this manner from an influx of illegal immigrants, and preserving its limited funds for use by individuals who are more likely to remain within the boundaries of the state. The majority accepted that the classification of alien children did not involve a suspect class and that the Equal Protection Clause permits the government "substantial latitude" that would require the Court to uphold such statutory classifications that are not arbitrarily discriminatory (*Id.*, p. 216). However, the Court simply did not find the government's actions rational. The Court did not permit discrimination against illegal alien children unless it furthered some substantial governmental goal. The ruling left only the dissent to argue that the legislation may not be wise but still sustainable because the state rationally could reach the conclusions that it did. *Plyler* serves as an example of a formally deferential and minimal review that ended up demanding.

The Court similarly rejected the government's actions as irrational, even if some rational arguments could support it, in *Cleburne v. Cleburne Living Center* (1985). *Cleburne* involved a challenge to a local zoning decision that denied a permit to construct a home for the mentally retarded. Applying rational basis review, the Supreme Court struck down the ordinance as applied to the center. The Court declined to rule that the mentally retarded constituted a suspect class on the grounds that they are a "large and diversified group" amply protected by state and federal legislatures (*Id.*, p. 442). However, in a unanimous opinion, the Court invalidated the ordinance as it held that the denial of the permit was based on irrational prejudice against the mentally retarded and that the rational basis test for legislative action provided sufficient protection against invidious discrimination. The city had argued, for example, that requiring a permit was necessary due to the negative attitude of the property owners who would be near the facility, fears of elderly residents of the neighborhood, and concern that the proposed center's being across the street from a junior high school would lead some students to harass the occupants. The Court was not persuaded, as it held that the record did not reveal any rational basis for believing that the center would pose any special threat to the city's legitimate interests.

The Court again rejected governmental actions on the grounds that they were irrational, and more famously so, in *Romer v. Evans* (1996). *Romer* involved an amendment to the Colorado state constitution ("Amendment 2") that would prevent any state-level governmental entity from recognizing gay and lesbian citizens as a protected class. The Court found that the amendment did not even pass the rational basis test, as it rejected the state's argument that the amendment merely blocked gay people from receiving special rights. Rather, the Court viewed the amendment as imposing a special disability on those persons alone; it viewed the statute as forbidding the safeguards that others enjoy or may seek without constraint. As such, the statute did not even meet the requirement of having a rational relationship to a legitimate government purpose, its sheer breadth was so discontinuous with the reasons offered for it that the amendment seemed inexplicable by anything but animosity toward the class that it affects, and the Court implied that the amendment simply was enacted to harm a politically unpopular group. The majority did not go into depth in rejecting the claims put forward in support of the law (protecting the rights of landlords to evict gay tenants if they found homosexuality morally offensive). The majority emphasized well how the Court can be flexible in its use of its own standards.

The dissenting opinion in *Romer* confirms the Court's flexibility. The dissenting justices found plenty of reasons to view the challenged law as rational. They viewed the amendment as not denying gay and lesbian individuals' access to the political process but merely as making it difficult to enact laws that they favored. They further noted that the Court previously had rejected a rational-basis challenge to sodomy laws on the grounds that traditional moral disapproval furnished such a rational basis. They also reasoned that the Constitution's silence on the subject (homosexuality) left its resolution to normal democratic means, including the democratic adoption of provisions in state constitutions. By striking down the amendment, the dissent argued, the Court was not acting on judicial judgment but on political will.

Importantly, *Romer* was taken as precedent in a more recent case, *Lawrence v. Texas* (2003). In *Lawrence*, the Court explicitly overturned its earlier *Bowers* (*Bowers v. Hardwick*, 1986) decision as it struck down sodomy laws as unconstitutional. However, the Court's analysis did not unequivocally reveal its applied level of scrutiny, even though the Court was dealing with similar classifications. Although the Court heeds to a variety of principles when deciding these issues, the line of cases remains revealing. It highlights how standards of review matter, but they only matter to an extent: Much depends on whether and how they will be applied.

The previous three examples reveal the Court's willingness to engage in a more rigorous and exacting review than typically would be expected under the rational basis standard of review. The Court supported what it viewed as strong individual interests at stake that outweighed the government's asserted interests. However, such swaying away from the typical application of the test results in questionable precedent. Notably, *Romer* has not been cited widely much beyond *Lawrence.* It was cited only once in passing, and not even in the legal analysis, in the more recent case involving same-sex marriage—a case that considered the equal protection challenge but focused more on the fundamental right to marry than on classifications based on biological sex (*Obergefell v. Hodges*, 2015). *Romer's* lack of precedental authority likely is due to the ruling opinion's emphasis on the "special" nature of Amendment 2 and its failure to apply the expected rational-basis analysis. These exceptional examples that come to unexpected ends could be viewed as the types that help confirm the general rule itself.

Moving away from exceptions and toward cases that have applied the rule as expected reveals the significance of the rational basis of review as well as the typical line of reasoning supporting it. Arguably the most illustrative cases involve challenges based on socioeconomic status and the use of public funds to support financially disadvantaged groups. These instances leave considerable discretion to the government, as illustrated in *San Antonio Independent School District v. Rodriguez* (1973).

Rodriguez involved a class action brought on behalf of Texas public school students who lived in school districts with a low property tax base. The differences in assessable property among districts caused substantial interdistrict disparities in tax burdens and per pupil expenditures, favoring richer districts. The students challenged the Texas school finance system as a violation of equal protection requirements of the Fourteenth Amendment. They asserted a right to equal educational opportunity, claiming that the amount spent per pupil should be the same throughout the state, and alleged that the Texas school financing plan resulted in inequality because more was being spent on students in richer districts even though their parents were taxed at lower rates. Applying the rational relationship standard and upholding the Texas method of public school finance, the Court concluded that there was a reasonable relationship between the state's educational obligations, the desire to allow local school district autonomy, and the Texas finance system. The Court used that low level of review on the grounds that the case involved neither fundamental interest (education of the children) nor suspect classifications (the discrimination against both children and parents in poorer school districts). By refusing to view wealth as the basis of a suspect classification, the Court gives districts the ability to make distinctions based on it.

The rational basis level of scrutiny leaves much for communities to decide. The approach leaves determinations of what constitutes equality or inequality to communities themselves because the classifications do not receive judicial protection. As long as the communities can justify their actions as rational, they essentially may leave entire classes of individuals unprotected and treat them differently from others. Although this approach to addressing equality may have been the subject of considerable derision, it now constitutes an area of hope to address inequality. It leaves to communities the ability to consider classifications in ways that enhance equality as much as they can exacerbate inequality.

Intermediate Scrutiny Review

The intermediate level of scrutiny arises from the need to deal with polar opposites. The rational basis review typically avoids a more searching and demanding review from courts for the simple reason that the government's classifications are not suspect, in that the classifications do not involve a protected class or a right deemed of fundamental importance. Governmental classifications that deal with highly protected classes or rights would lead to a court's use of its strictest scrutiny, as it thus would be dealing with what is deemed inherently suspect classifications. However, only a small number of rights and classifications are granted the highest protection. A wide range of classifications and rights fall within these two poles. As expected, the Court has recognized, almost haphazardly, a set of quasi-suspect classifications that undergo intermediate review. The Court requires such reviews to distinguish among reasonable, substantial, and close relationships between the classification and the state's interest at stake, and reviews also must determine the weight to be given to the governmental interest at stake. As with other areas of law, a few cases can illustrate well the nature of this level of review and its implications.

The conception of intermediate scrutiny formally dates from the 1970s to cases in which the government's actions classified people based on their sex. The leading case that developed and adopted this standard of review was *Craig v. Boren* (1976). In that case, the Court invalidated an Oklahoma law that distinguished between men and women in setting the drinking age for certain low-alcohol beverages. Thought to be responding to a growing conviction that differential treatment of women and men created social problems rather than to a conviction that women were an insular minority that could not participate effectively in the political process, the Court declared that distinctions on the basis of gender are "quasi-suspect" and must face "intermediate scrutiny." Reflecting the intermediate nature of this form of judicial scrutiny, the Court reasoned that intermediate scrutiny requires that a challenged law "substantially advance an important state interest" (*Craig v. Boren*, 1976, p. 197). That interest need not be a compelling one, but the government must have reason to interfere in the protected group's rights.

Later, in *Mississippi University for Women v. Hogan* (1982, p. 724), the Court further clarified the standard as it ruled that the burden is on the proponent of the classification to establish an "exceedingly persuasive justification" to validate a sex-based classification. The burden is met only by showing at least that the classification serves "important governmental objectives, and that the discriminatory means employed" are "substantially related to the achievement of those objectives" (*Id.*, pp. 723–724). In that case, Hogan was denied admission to a baccalaureate degree program in nursing at the university. Except for his being male, he was qualified. Although denied admission, he was offered the opportunity to audit classes. The school argued that the state had two other nursing programs that he could attend, although both were more than 100 miles away. Hogan challenged the single-sex admissions policy.

The Court in *Hogan* applied intermediate scrutiny as it noted that the government had not advanced an important state interest for operating a single-sex nursing school, especially given that other institutions trained female nurses and that the school was actually not single sex because males were permitted to audit nursing classes. Without an important state objective supporting the differential treatment of women (providing them differential access to the nursing program), the distinction based on sex was illegitimate, particularly because it tended to perpetuate inappropriate sex-based stereotypes. Permitting males to attend classes meant that the state's gender-based classification did not directly relate to its proposed compensatory objective; excluding men was not necessary for the school to reach its goals because men already were permitted in the classroom. A strong dissent argued that Hogan had not suffered a cognizable injury because he could attend other programs in the state and the state was offering programs to men, that there was no constitutional right to attend a state-supported university in one's home town, and that a state could offer its citizens the legitimate choice to attend single-sex institutions. The majority found the dissent's points unpersuasive, as *Hogan* not only confirmed the increased protection against gender distinctions but also revealed, by giving protections to males, the importance of classifications regardless of the gender historically subordinated.

The Court in the previous cases applied intermediate scrutiny in a way closer to strict scrutiny. In more recent decisions involving gender, the Court has preferred the term "exacting scrutiny" when referring to the intermediate level of Equal Protection analysis. Two examples are illustrative.

The first example, *J.E.B. v. Alabama* (1994), involved Alabama's prosecution of a civil case against J.E.B. for child support. To favor its case, Alabama used its peremptory strikes to exclude male jurors from the jury so that the resulting jury was all female. The Court previously had held that a state could not use its peremptory strikes to exclude jurors solely on the basis of race (a highly protected class). The Court extended that protection to gender and ruled that the Constitution's guarantee of equal protection under the Fourteenth Amendment forbids intentional discrimination on the basis of gender, just as it prohibits discrimination on the basis of race. It reasoned that "gender-based classifications require 'an exceedingly persuasive justification' in order to survive constitutional scrutiny. Parties still may remove jurors whom they feel might be less acceptable than others on the panel; gender simply may not serve as a proxy for bias" (*Id.*, p. 143). It further found that excluding jurors based on gender "sends the message that certain individuals, for no reason other than gender, are presumed to be unqualified by State actors to decide important questions upon which reasonable persons could disagree" (*Id.*, p. 142). Similar to *Hogan*, the Court protected gender as a classification to restrict discrimination against men, and it did so by putting the state to the task of providing much more than rational justifications for treating the sexes differently.

The other illustrative case is *United States v. Virginia* (1996). In that case, the Court struck down the long-standing male-only admission policy of the Virginia Military Institute (VMI). The majority found that because it failed to show an "exceedingly persuasive justification" for its sex-based admissions policy, VMI violated the Fourteenth Amendment's Equal Protection Clause (*Id.*, p. 531). Importantly, Virginia had proposed a parallel program for women, called the Virginia Women's Institute for Leadership (VWIL), located at Mary Baldwin College, a private liberal arts women's college. However, the Court held that VWIL would not provide women with the same type of rigorous military training, facilities, courses, faculty, financial opportunities, and/or alumni reputation and connections that VMI affords male cadets—a decision evocative of *Sweatt v. Painter* (1950). In *Sweatt*, the Court had ruled segregated law schools in Texas unconstitutional partly on the grounds that a newly formed Black law school clearly did not provide the same benefits to its students as the state's prestigious and long-maintained White law school. Despite using a higher standard of review and evoking parallels to impermissible racial classifications that gain the highest scrutiny, the opinion for the Court used neither the strict scrutiny standard nor the intermediate one because its language did not comport with the important governmental interest formula used in prior intermediate scrutiny cases.

A stinging dissenting opinion in the VMI case argued that the standard applied by the majority was closer to a strict scrutiny standard than the intermediate scrutiny standard applied to previous cases involving equal protection based on sex. It also went one step further and reasoned that neither of those standards was appropriate. Justice Scalia argued that

> if the question of the applicable standard of review for sex-based classifications were to be regarded as an appropriate subject for reconsideration, the stronger argument would be not for elevating the standard to strict scrutiny, but for reducing it to rational-basis review. (*United States v. Virginia*, 1996, p. 575)

With the VMI decision, the Court effectively struck down any law that, as Justice Ginsburg wrote, "denies to women, simply because they are women, full citizenship stature—equal opportunity to aspire, achieve, participate in and contribute to society" (*Id.*, p. 532). The Court's decision may have been protective of gender classifications, then, but the case reflects the less than settled view of the nature of that protection.

In addition to not clearly agreeing on and articulating standards and rationales for protecting gender classifications, the VMI decision left much more unanswered. For example, whether a gender classification supporting sex-based admissions in public schooling would survive equal protection challenges remains an open question. The decision did not resolve whether the separate but equal approach to gendered education remains lawful because Virginia offered a patently inferior alternative to women it excluded from VMI. In fact, Chief Justice Rehnquist had written a concurrence to highlight and defend the possibility of separate single-sex schools. He noted that it was the maintenance of an all-men school without providing a comparable institution for women that was problematic; the exclusion of women itself did not violate the Equal Protection Clause. Notably, the Court did not make any reference to *Brown*. The Court had chosen, instead, to focus on contrasting Virginia's approach to single-sex schools that dissipate, rather than perpetuate, traditional gender classifications. The Court had gone so far as to note the uncontested notion that single-sex education afforded pedagogical benefits to some students. How the Court will resolve these issues remains to be seen, but for now, indications are that gender classifications do receive intermediate protection in comparison to, for example, racial classifications.

Gender classifications do not stand alone in receiving intermediate scrutiny. The Court also subjects restrictions based on illegitimacy to intermediate scrutiny in the Equal Protection context. *Reed v. Campbell* (1986) illustrates its use. In that case, a child was born to a marriage that was deemed invalid because the father already was married to another woman. The Court reaffirmed a long line of cases that unambiguously had concluded that a state may not justify discriminatory treatment of illegitimates in order to express its disapproval of their parents' misconduct. Courts have found that imposing legal burdens on illegitimate persons in order to express disapproval of the conduct of their parents is illogical, unjust, and contrary to the fundamental principle that legal burdens should have some relationship to individual wrongdoing. The Court did note a permissible basis for some distinctions made partly on the basis of legitimacy, such as when a statutory provision has an evident and substantial relationship to the state's interest in providing for the orderly and just distribution of a decedent's property at death, particularly the state interest in finality. The Court found no similar justification or compelling reason to treat illegitimate children when those interests were not at issue.

The courts have found such scrutiny necessary for a number of reasons. Like race or gender, the Court has stressed that an illegitimate person's status of birth is a condition over which individuals have no control, and it has no bearing on their ability or willingness to contribute to society. In applying increasingly exacting intermediate scrutiny, the courts have noted that illegitimate persons are a stigmatized minority, are vastly outnumbered politically, and are the target of long-standing and continuing invidious legal discrimination. For all these reasons, the Court mandates exacting constitutional scrutiny under the Equal Protection Clause of the Fourteenth Amendment. How and whether these special protections will continue given demographic changes in marital patterns remains to be seen, especially given that illegitimacy does not appear in the Constitution as a protected classification. That potential for change highlights the importance and nature of intermediate scrutiny.

Conclusions

During the past several decades, the most important doctrinal development in the jurisprudence of constitutional rights has been the formulation and proliferation of "tiers of scrutiny" that the courts use to balance individual liberties with societal needs. The Supreme Court formalized this area of jurisprudence to reconcile the general presumption of constitutionality and deference to legislative bodies with the inherently countermajoritarian nature of judicial review. Originally, the Court created two tiers to structure constitutional analyses of challenged governmental actions: the highly deferential rational basis review and the almost always "fatal in fact" strict scrutiny. Rooted in the Court's due process and equal protection jurisprudence, these modes of analysis developed and now figure prominently throughout the Court's constitutional rights jurisprudence.

The previously discussed developments in jurisprudence have become central to addressing differential treatment based on one's group status. The developments mean that the government may differentiate individuals along group classifications and, based on those classifications, treat them differently. Some classifications may not receive much protection, making them open to differential treatment, whereas some will receive heightened scrutiny prohibiting differential treatment. By engaging in a series of searching analyses, courts determine whether the law can so easily differentiate and differently treat classifications deemed "suspect." Primary determinations focus on whether the goals supporting differentiation rise to the level of a compelling governmental interest. If a compelling governmental interest is needed, as in when applying strict scrutiny analysis, and if that interest is identified, the question becomes whether the government's actions further that compelling interest in a manner that is tailored narrowly to achieving it. If the judiciary does not view the classifications as suspect, then the classifications are not highly protected and the government has more freedom to make and use them.

The previously discussed developments in how the courts review the legitimacy of governmental actions influence the potential relevance and utility of empirical evidence. These analyses all lend themselves to considerations of empirical formulations and findings. Empirical evidence becomes relevant to demonstrating whether compelling interests exist and whether the government's proposed actions appropriately reach (or could reach) those interests. In addition, empirical evidence becomes important in devising neutral alternatives to the classifications deemed inappropriate either because they do not further a compelling enough governmental interest or because the policies were implemented inappropriately in furtherance of an acceptable governmental interest. Empirical evidence can help uncover the legitimacy of the government's rationales when its actions differentially impact different groups. Similarly, empirical evidence can help identify ways to reach articulated goals without even using classifications. Chapter 3 examines the nature of the compelling interests that the Court has either accepted or rejected as important to consider when the government seeks to treat people differently based on their racial/ethnic status.

3

Legal Rationales Relating to School Segregation and Diversity

The Need for a Comprehensive Examination of Rationales

The US Constitution's Fourteenth Amendment protects the right to be treated equally. It explicitly declares that no state shall deny any person within its jurisdiction "the equal protection of the laws." However, that right does not apply to everything that the government does. Exceptions to the mandate of equal treatment routinely arise, and the Court has developed ways to address whether and how the legal system must treat members of particular groups the same as members of other groups.

To determine the legitimacy of the government's group-based classifications, the Court subjects them to various levels of scrutiny. When dealing with racial classifications, analyses center on the extent to which the government retains a compelling interest in asserting a need for differential treatment. If the reasons for differential treatment are deemed compelling enough to pursue, the Court also considers the extent to which the government's actions appropriately reach the intended goals of furthering compelling interests. Equally important, even if the government's actions happen to treat groups differently, that difference does not matter unless the government intentionally made group-based distinctions. Neutral laws avoid close scrutiny and have a presumption of legitimacy. This means that laws are legitimate if they just so happen to disadvantage one group, even a highly protected group. However, laws attract close scrutiny to ensure their legitimacy when they classify individuals based on protected characteristics, such as race.

How the judiciary scrutinizes governmental actions is clear, but it invites disagreement. Members of the Supreme Court do agree about the standards used to hold the government accountable for protecting individuals' rights to equal treatment regardless of race. However, they often disagree about which part of that standard to apply, the factors to be considered, the relative weight to be given to them, and even when situations call for the use of specific standards.

The previously mentioned disagreements have real consequences. For example, four dissenting justices in *Parents Involved in Community Schools v. Seattle School District No. 1* (2007) would permit school districts to use race-conscious plans and scrutinize such measures under a standard less stringent than traditional strict scrutiny. They argue that traditional strict scrutiny applies to exclusionary uses of racial classifications and that a more lenient form of strict scrutiny should apply when race-conscious plans are beneficial or seek to include people in a benefit on the basis of their race. To them, the Constitution "permits local school boards to use race-conscious criteria to achieve positive race-related goals, even when the Constitution does not compel it" (p. 823). If the justices can disagree about the threshold determination of when to apply a well-recognized standard, it should not be surprising that they disagree about its application and the resolution of disputes before them. It also means that their disagreements will influence whether and how they will embrace empirical evidence to support their decisions.

How members of the Court address these issues generally depends on whether they adopt anti-classification or anti-subordination approaches. As previously discussed, neither of these approaches leads to predetermined outcomes, but each one furthers different views of the legal system's role in creating and addressing harms from differential treatment. And justices do not consistently embrace one approach over another; nor do they fully follow either approach that they do embrace. Still, generally, the anti-classification approach permits the use of differential treatment in a narrow set of circumstances, whereas the anti-subordination approach supports more differential treatment to shape different outcomes—one approach is color-blind, whereas the other is color-conscious. This means that arguments about whether to permit the government to treat people differently based on race rest on different interpretations of what constitutes appropriate compelling interests, as well as on what the government can do to tailor its remedies narrowly.

Whether the legal system can intentionally treat individuals from different racial groups differently, then, turns on reasons for doing so and how the government seeks to further them. This means that empirical analyses of the appropriateness of differential treatment must address the potential reasons for and against the law's use of classifications and their actual use. Empirical research may be up to the task, but its potential role in influencing legal matters nevertheless raises important concerns. Caution must be used when identifying and responding to the law's empirical needs because the legal system does not always respond to empirical reality or reflect people's experiences. That possibility makes it important to begin with a thorough analysis of the law's potential needs.

Potential Rationales for Treating People Differently Because of Their Race/Ethnicity

The Supreme Court has long grappled with justifications for treating individuals differently because of their group status. The most persuasive rationale for explicitly and directly treating people differently by race involves using racial classifications to remedy the legal system's own intentional discrimination and the harms that come from it. Other justifications focus on the negative outcomes associated with general societal discrimination, such as feelings of inferiority, negative health, and limited economic opportunities that result from differential treatment. Yet other justifications center on the failure to achieve positive outcomes, such as the academic and social benefits that arise from diverse learning environments as well as the manner in which diverse environments empower individuals to live in a pluralistic society and support democracy itself.

Each of the previously mentioned rationales for treating individuals differently because of their racial/ethnic status has been considered in the educational context. And, as expected, not everyone is in agreement about their persuasiveness and relevance. Each rationale has its own strengths and weaknesses, and each raises different empirical challenges. How the legal system frames these rationales determines the potential utility of empirical analyses.

Remedying Past Discrimination

The need to remedy the vestiges of intentional discrimination by the government constitutes the most readily recognized compelling interest for treating individuals from highly protected groups differently. The significance of this interest has been made clear from *Brown* to *Parents Involved*. A need to remedy past governmental actions, when the remedy is narrowly tailored, survives strict scrutiny and is deemed permissible. The compelling interest—the need to remedy past problematic legal actions—arguably serves as the strongest reason to support the government's use of race-based classifications to treat people differently.

The need to remedy past discrimination involves several empirical assertions. The Court requires a showing that the differential treatment remains necessary. This position was stated directly by Justice Thomas, as he concluded that a governmental entity must establish "a strong basis in evidence for its conclusion that remedial action was necessary" (*Parents Involved*, 2007, p. 754). To establish that strong basis, the entity must (1) address the extent of its past discrimination, (2) address the scope of any injury and the necessary remedy, and (3) demonstrate that the remedy addresses "more than inherently unmeasurable claims of past wrongs" (*Id.*, p. 755). In other words, the government cannot simply assert an interest in remediation that will treat people differently because of their race; the government must assert "a strong basis in evidence" to show past discrimination and demonstrate that the present effects of the discrimination require race-conscious remediation measures. The heavy evidentiary burden helps ensure that the government seeks genuine remedial goals given the need to proceed cautiously when treating people differently because of their racial status.

The compelling interest in remedying past invidious discrimination by the government may be strong, but it has important limitations. The focus on the government's invidious discrimination and the need for a remedy rejects other potential reasons for differential treatment. In addition, it also limits the utility of empirical evidence offered to support remedies.

As *Parents Involved* makes clear, a majority on the Supreme Court dismisses what others might view as compelling interests to remedy past harms of discrimination. Under *Parents Involved*, a school district does not have a compelling interest to remedy the present effect of past discrimination if a district has never been subject to a court-ordered desegregation decree. Nor does the school district have a compelling reason if it previously had a decree to desegregate but no longer is under the mandate. Nor can the district seek to remedy past discrimination if its policies had not segregated its schools. Without those conditions, the government does not retain an interest to address past discrimination because the discrimination that matters to the legal system does not exist.

The need to require past governmental differentiated treatment is quite revealing and has important consequences for the use of empirical evidence. The focus on the government's actions highlights how a school district cannot argue a compelling interest in preventing resegregation and a school cannot use racial imbalance, in and of itself, to support a compelling interest argument. A sharp distinction exists between segregation and racial imbalance. Segregation in the public school context arises when the school system deliberately carries out a government policy to separate students in schools solely on the basis of their race. By contrast, racial imbalance refers to school districts' failure to create schools that match or approximate the demographic makeup of the student population at large. Although racial imbalance might be the result of de jure (intentional) segregation, it also might be caused by private decision-making. Given that it need not link inevitably to unconstitutional segregation, racial imbalance need not be unconstitutional in and of itself. Thus, schools may be in danger of racial imbalance but not necessarily of resegregation; the legal system deems racial imbalances not directly caused by governmental policies as unfortunate side effects of racially neutral educational decision-making. In other words, just as a school cannot desegregate a system that it did not initially segregate, a school cannot remedy discrimination unless the law recognizes the initial discrimination.

The fundamental lesson that results from these legal rules is that much of what researchers identify as problematic racial imbalances result from neutral laws that do not directly consider race. The legal system prohibits the use of racial classifications to change those imbalances. Under these circumstances, no amount of evidence of racial imbalance can support a remedy if it is legally irrelevant. Showing that individuals from minority groups are likely to be educated with other members of their group, which researchers often offer as evidence of discrimination, is not necessarily evidence of discrimination that the legal system can directly remedy.

Remedying Governmental Discrimination

In addition to remedying the vestiges of past discrimination, the government has an interest in addressing some of the effects of that discrimination. For example, the government arguably has a compelling interest beyond the feelings of inferiority it generates in denying equal treatment to one group of citizens; it has an interest in the harmful effects that feelings of inferiority generate. In the context of *Brown* (*Brown v. Board of Education*, 1954), for example, the effects relate to equal access to educational quality:

> The impact [of segregation] is greater when it has the sanction of the law; for the policy of separating the races is usually interpreted as denoting the inferiority of the negro group. A sense of inferiority affects the motivation of a child to learn. Segregation with the sanction of law, therefore, has a tendency to retard the educational and mental development of negro children and to deprive them of some of the benefits they would receive in a racially integrated school system. (p. 494)

Brown makes clear that the government has an interest in not depriving minority children of equal educational opportunities. Finding that a productive life depends on access to quality education, the Court questioned whether any child could succeed in life without educational opportunities.

Thus, under *Brown*, segregation is harmful because it generates feelings of inferiority in minority children, which negatively impacts their motivation to learn and impairs their mental development. It was this reasoning that led to the abolishment of segregated schools—the reasoning that segregated schools cannot offer high-quality education to minority students. In short, laws cannot create "separate but equal" schools. The Court found separated schools inherently unequal because segregation itself disrupts the hearts and minds of minority students in a way that must impact their prospects for academic success.

As currently interpreted by the Supreme Court in *Parents Involved*, the Court's analysis in *Brown* centered on the effects of the laws themselves. It focused on the laws rather than on racial imbalances and lack of opportunities not tied directly to the government's actions. The law itself had caused the harm. Having a law that directly causes a specific harm provides a compelling reason to remedy that harm, even if it means treating people differently by race.

The compelling interest in addressing the harms that the legal system caused to individuals' sense of self may make several empirical claims. The most important ones include the need to demonstrate that the harm actually occurs. If the harm does occur, then research can guide the types of remedies to address them. However, the relevance of the empirical record may be contentious depending on different views about the legal system's role in causing the harm. Was the harm the legal system's different treatment of individuals based on race? That the races were educated separately? That the separate educations were problematic due to different resources? These questions end up mattering in that they determine what type of remedies, if any, can address the individual harms.

The legal system itself will determine the relevance of research. If the Court decides to take a narrow view of harm, it may well render empirical research irrelevant because the real concern would be the use of racial classifications; once racial classifications are eliminated, then so would the harms. Another view might be that harm lingers and requires continued remedies, which requires empirical evaluation. Again, the law's framing of issues matters.

Remedying Legal Actions

The government may have a compelling interest to remedy its own discrimination and that discrimination's related harms, but which legal actions count as discrimination is debatable. The accepted approach takes a narrow view and centers on direct action. This is what *Parents Involved* meant, for example, when the Court focused on the legal system's classifications. Anti-classifications approaches require direct governmental action as a foundation for fashioning remedies. Without initial governmental action that would cause unequal treatment, the legal system generally cannot be part of potential remedies. This view makes significant what actually can fall under the umbrella of governmental action because research findings simply run the risk of irrelevance in the absence of direct state action causing the differential treatment effects under study. Thus, and following this line of legal reasoning, regardless of the amount of research conducted in this area, much of it potentially remains irrelevant.

In *Parents Involved*, Justice Roberts essentially finds empirical evidence either not relevant to doctrine or, if it would happen to become relevant, unpersuasive. A narrow view of governmental action, one that would focus on the specific policy that directly classifies individuals based on race, makes for a relatively simple empirical inquiry. In fact, not much need exists for an inquiry in the first instance, as demonstrating the existence of an inappropriate legal classification based on race suffices for demonstrating that the government retains a compelling interest to remedy it. Absent that classification, the government simply must not classify based on race. This approach, which reaches decisions simply based on whether incidents are allocated in particular categories, vitiates the need for any deep empirical analysis.

Given this view, Chief Justice Roberts' opinion did not cite support from empirical research or any of the social science briefs. In addition, even if there would be a need to turn to empirical evidence—that is, if the Court were to adopt a more expansive approach to determining the grounds for a compelling governmental interest—he still was not persuaded that the evidence would shed appropriate light as he noted that "[t]he parties and their amici dispute whether racial diversity in schools in fact has a marked impact on test scores and other objective yardsticks or achieves intangible socialization benefits" (*Parents Involved*, 2007, p. 726). Requiring consensus among social scientists certainly sets a high bar—one not often reached given that the scientific enterprise, by its very nature, involves questioning findings. Turning to empirical findings likely would be unhelpful, then, given both conflicting findings and the legal grounds that would make them relevant.

The legal system, however, can lead to discrimination indirectly by creating contexts that contribute to disparities. Examples include policies relating to housing (creating and locating public housing within specific districts) and financial support for schools (relying on property tax assessments) that relates to schools' effectiveness as well as where groups of children likely will attend school (Mickelson, 2003). These are the types of arguments adopted by anti-subordination approaches suggesting that systemic effects of entire systems of law, rather than discrete and direct legal actions, contribute to disparities.

The direct or indirect nature of legal actions raises empirical matters. Unlike other rationales for treating people differently to remedy past actions, the legal system forms ways that make searching empirical analyses irrelevant—either the legal system uses race to classify or not. However, that simple analysis need not be so simple. Can the indirect governmental actions be shown to create disparities? Can laws that appear neutral be shown to create disparities? For those who experience disparities, does it matter whether the government does so directly or indirectly?

The previously mentioned types of empirical concerns are important because of the way that the legal system creates remedies. Neutral laws can be used to address disparities. However, the very fact that they are being used suggests that classifications are being used. Justice Kennedy noted important examples of particularly neutral ways to alleviate racial disparities, but he was joined by no other justice. The approaches may well address disparities, but it is difficult to escape the use of race. Using a proxy for race, such as poverty or location, does not avoid the use of race as it simply uses it indirectly. Again, even embarking on these types of remedies is particularly problematic because recognition of the need for a remedy only comes after recognizing and making racial classifications. Empirical analyses may shed light on some of these concerns, but whether they will influence the legal system remains to be seen.

Enhancing Diversity

Moving beyond the government's own actions, arguments have been made that governments have a compelling interest in the diversity of a school's student body. The Court had recognized that interest in *Grutter v. Bollinger* (2003) in the context of higher education on the grounds that student diversity was vital to the law school's educational mission. A majority of the Supreme Court's justices in *Parents Involved*, however, rejected that compelling interest as applied to schools other than colleges and universities. The key rationale supporting that distinction between university and lower levels of education was the "expansive freedoms of speech and thought associated with the university environment" and the belief that "universities occupy a special niche in our constitutional tradition" (*Grutter v. Bollinger*, 2003, p. 329). In addition, the law school had sought to further that compelling interest in a narrowly tailored manner. The *Grutter* plan had used a "highly individualized, holistic review" (*Id.*, p. 337) of applicants rather than making race a determining factor, which also was a reason that the Court had rejected the use of race in *Gratz v. Bollinger, Grutter's* companion case that had focused on university admissions. The school assignment plans in *Parents Involved* had made race a determining factor and had failed to articulate how they could fall in the special niche carved for universities.

In *Parents Involved*, however, some of the justices who had rejected this justification left it open for later consideration. One of the key opinions was not averse to race-based assignments if primary and secondary schools could demonstrate that diversity constitutes a compelling educational goal. This was an important point that some other justices also seemed opened to consider as they noted that the schools in *Parents Involved* had not made strong pedagogical arguments for differential treatment based on race. Notably, for example, Justice Roberts had remarked that both school assignment plans in *Parents Involved* were exclusively focused on achieving demographic goals and not toward achieving any benefit of racial diversity. Room may exist for arguing that a pedagogical need for diversity can support a compelling interest for differential treatment.

Justifying differential treatment to enhance diversity leads to the tricky task of arguing for diversity's benefits. That argument would need to be based on diversity's effects on social and academic outcomes and demonstrate how other alternatives simply do not allow for achieving those benefits. The Court in *Parents Involved* (2007, p. 726) had concluded that it did not need to resolve the dispute "whether diversity in schools in fact has a marked impact on test scores and other intangible . . . socialization benefits" because the challenged school assignment plans were not narrowly tailored to achieve the educational and social benefits that would result from such diversity. The school districts had not tied their policies to any pedagogic concept that might determine the level of diversity needed to attain the asserted educational benefits of diversity. Rather, the plans were linked only to the racial demographics of each school district. The focus on racial demographics, without a clear consideration of the rationale that would support it, rendered the use of classifications impermissible. The Court's explicitly setting aside the issue leaves open the possibility that demonstrating the benefits of diversity may be persuasive enough to result in a close consideration of a compelling interest argument based on diversity's social and academic benefits.

The potential compelling interest in social and academic benefits of diversity may be demonstrable, but doing so likely will remain challenging. The dissent in *Parents Involved* argued that the districts had a compelling interest in using the school assignment policies, based on race, to achieve educational goals. The argument was that the educational element represented school districts' "interest in overcoming the adverse educational effects produced by and associated with highly segregated schools" (*Id.*, p. 839). That argument was not deemed persuasive enough even in light of the very close consideration that the dissent gave to available empirical evidence. The ruling opinions simply did not view the available evidence as sufficiently convincing.

Even if diversity could be accepted as a compelling interest supported by empirical research, policies furthering its implementation must be tailored narrowly. Doing so likely will be difficult. The Court clearly stated that to be tailored narrowly, the assignment plans needed a "logical stopping point" (*Id.*, p. 731). In *Parents Involved*, as the demographics of the districts would shift, so would the racial guidelines of the plans. To complicate matters, it would be difficult to determine the diversity needed to achieve the purported social and academic benefits that come from diversity. Also, the need to determine how much diversity raises the specter of arguing for quotas, an argument that the Court long ago rejected (*Regents of the University of California v. Bakke*, 1978). Without doubt, commentators may accept diversity as a compelling interest, but turning that interest into a concept that the courts will accept, and then articulating policies to implement it, remains challenging. That challenge, however, raises numerous empirical issues important to address given their potential legal relevance.

Remedying Societal Discrimination

In determining the need to treat individuals differently based on race, the Court has addressed the possible compelling interest in remedying general societal discrimination. An argument can be made that the use of racial classifications is necessary to address the effects of societal discrimination that eventually leads to having schools with disproportionate percentages of students from different racial groups. For example, the Seattle plan in *Parents Involved* (2007) was adopted partly to address the consequences of racial housing patterns, given that those led to the schools' different racial balances. The Court explicitly held that such use of racial classifications would be inappropriate on the grounds that racial classifications cannot be used to remedy general societal discrimination. The Court's position that general societal discrimination has no constitutional implications for supporting governmental interests in differential treatment has deep roots in the educational context. This line of reasoning seeks to increase precision in the remedy that the racial classification means to address, and it also reveals the need for direct links arguably supported by empirical evidence. General societal discrimination simply is too general; remedies for a particular problem need more particularized causes that can be linked directly to specific remedies.

That the Court addressed this issue at all reveals its significance. The racial disparities found in society are the ones that attract people's attention and figure prominently in empirical analyses. Many types of disparities influence where children go to school, how well they do in school, the nature of available resources, and the extent to which they benefit from them. These include housing decisions, socioeconomic status, family patterns, and commitment to education. Despite the tendency to link these disparities to societal forces and general discrimination, the legal system does not view it that way. The legal system deems these concerns as involving de facto discrimination. These disparities are the type that the legal system attributes mainly to private choices, and private discrimination, outside of the government's direct actions. No matter how often communities seek to treat groups differently to address these disparities in experiences, the legal system rejects their efforts. Similarly, no matter how much evidence supports the existence of these disparities in experiences, the legal system does not support using them as rationales to treat people differently by race. That lack of support means that, at the very least, researchers need to rethink how to package their findings differently and ask different questions about them.

Securing Democratic Ideals

A last compelling interest presented as potentially supporting the use of racial classifications involves society's interest in democracy. *Brown*, for example, had revealed an interest in producing an educational element that reflects the pluralistic society in which children will live. *Parents Involved* (2007, pp. 867–868) had raised a similar argument as it viewed *Brown's* promise "of true racial equality . . . as a matter of everyday life in the Nation's cities and schools." Also, recently, the Court has accepted the rationale that schools have an interest in cultivating leaders with legitimacy in the eyes of the citizenry (*Fisher II; Fisher v. the University of Texas at Austin*, 2016). The argument is that our pluralistic society values and needs public school systems that prepare students for life in an integrated, pluralistic society.

Although frequently evoked, the interest raises several issues. The argument lacks the precision typically required by this area of law. Determining the balance that would be found in society's future may involve precision that cannot be achieved, particularly in light of the challenge of not being able to determine the appropriate balance needed to reach purported educational and academic benefits. Still, the compelling interest continues to be identified and, as such, raises important empirical issues. Is society actually pluralistic? If so, then how so? Does pluralism need to be fostered by the government? Regardless of whether society is pluralistic, does its pluralism need to be different from its current manifestation? How can youth be prepared to live in the articulated type of pluralistic society? What role does formal education play? What is absolutely necessary for youth to live in such a society? The same types of questions relate to democratic ideals.

The Court may be open to considering the previous types of evidence to determine the persuasiveness of the rationale that our pluralistic and democratic society demands racial equality. But that does not determine the legal system's potential role in achieving it. Research may indicate a compelling need, but it may not necessarily support acceptable ways of treating people differently to address them. Cases dealing with education frequently laud its role in democracy and society. Such statements may invite empirical analyses, but those analyses may not be the type that the legal system requires. Some legal justifications may rest more on political ideals and broadly accepted facts that do not need empirical support.

Potential Rationales for Not Treating People Differently Based on Their Race

The government may have compelling interests to classify individuals into protected categories, but such interests may be countered by other interests that support not doing so. These are critical to understand. Analyses of equal treatment must consider rationales for not treating differently individuals who fall into different group classifications. Many of the reasons for not pursuing compelling interests in treating groups differently relate to procedural issues—for example, the challenges of narrowly tailoring the differential treatment in a manner that would not inappropriately infringe on other rights or the challenges of identifying an appropriate percentage of diversity to further a compelling interest in diverse student bodies. However, other types of arguments go beyond issues of implementation. These types of arguments challenge the nature of compelling interests. Essentially, they argue countervailing concerns for not pursuing even compelling reasons for using racial status to treat people differently. Legal systems must consider these types of substantive concerns as much as procedural ones, particularly because these concerns tend to be entangled.

Several general and specific concerns emerge when the legal system treats individuals differently due to their group status. General concerns that dominate legal analyses typically distill to two risks: the hazards associated with promoting a sense of group inferiority (e.g., through stigma) and the risks of creating hostility among groups. In addition, concerns can relate to broader issues involving the allocation of governmental responsibilities—determining the appropriate level of government to address issues of equality by balancing between leaving matters to local communities or federal courts, which balances granting power to those with relevant experience and expertise against those who can take a broader view of needs and spread resources. Added to these general concerns are those relating to the specific area of differential treatment, such as the failure to benefit from a specific service provided by the government, with the most litigated one being educational harms that result from lack of access to educational opportunities. As expected, these concerns do not necessarily dictate a specific resolution regarding the pursuit of compelling interests, a point that provides yet another reason for proceeding with caution when pursuing governmental interests. Still, all these concerns need close attention because they figure prominently in efforts to address inequality and raise important empirical questions.

Avoiding Stigma

One of the most forcefully articulated and accepted concerns relating to the legal system's distinguishing among groups and treating them differently relates to the stigma and sense of inferiority that can arise from the government's differentiation. This was, for example, a key issue in cases addressing race-based policies: the concern that the laws promoted group inferiority. Advantaging members of one group may be perceived or experienced as disadvantaging members of other groups. By denoting one group's superiority, the classification reinforces the subordination of the other.

The process of governmental stigmatization was well articulated in *Brown*. In that case, the Court had held that governmental classification and separation on grounds of race denoted inferiority. The law's role in creating this sense of inferiority ran deep and had a long history. Segregation before *Brown* existed to exclude Blacks from full and equal participation in society by labeling them and defining them as inferior. The goal was to stigmatize and subordinate, so as to limit the social, political, and economic mobility of Blacks, as exemplified by "Jim Crow" laws that served as a reminder of the inferior status of Blacks. The subordination permitted Whites' advantages and sense that others were inferior. *Brown* resolved the matter by prohibiting the use of race as the sole determinant of children's school assignments mostly on the rationale that the law breeds a sense of inferiority when it treats individuals according to group classifications such as race.

The government's classifications based on group status, however, may not necessarily create a sense of disadvantage or inferiority. Classifications may have the opposite effect. Some classifications that result in differential treatment could be used to address the harms associated with the classification: They may dissipate rather than perpetuate harmful stereotypes and classifications. This point has been raised in the context of education. For example, special identity schools (e.g., based on race, sex, language, and sexual orientation) may help counter the development of a sense of inferiority that could arise from being in situations in which they would be treated similarly to others. Exclusive identity schools may provide environments in which students feel better cared for as well as believed in, and in which they can learn safely from harms of low expectations, harassment, or prejudice.

These efforts seek to account for racial differences and justify special identity schools for the purposes of fostering pride, remedying past disadvantages, and preparing youth for a still discriminatory world.

Concern for stigma also emerges in other ways. Remedies for past inappropriate treatment can include what has become known as reverse discrimination. Individuals may well feel disadvantaged and stigmatized without cause when treated differently so that others can be treated better to undo past wrongful actions. These situations emerge, for example, when individuals do not feel individually responsible for the government's prior actions but are now deprived on the basis of their own race. Being wronged to make up for someone else's wrongs smacks as unfair. Disadvantage creates subjugation and problematic feelings that accompany it.

The different repercussions that come from addressing past harms raise important concerns for this area of jurisprudence. They provide an important example of how legal assumptions may not play out in real life. They also reveal how empirical analyses actually can shed light on the legal system's efforts. The legal system must adopt one stance over another. Some stances may fail to achieve goals as well as others. The identification of these situations and nuances provides the type of evidence that the legal system needs to develop effectively.

Avoiding Group Hostility

Another concern relating to differential treatment involves the risk of spawning hostility among classified groups. Concerns about harmony have long been central to jurisprudence relating to race-conscious policies. In *Parents Involved* (2007, for example, Chief Justice Roberts contended that such propensity could "reinforce the belief . . . that individuals should be judged by the color of their skin," which then could lead to "a Nation divided into racial blocs, thus contributing to an escalation of racial hostility and conflict" (pp. 746–747). Following that reasoning to its conclusion, Roberts asserted that absent a judicial remedial order, any use of race threatened racial harmony. This line of reasoning culminated in the overall proposition that "[t]he way to stop discrimination on the basis of race is to stop discriminating on the basis of race" (*Id.*, p. 748). Also in *Parents Involved*, Justice Kennedy warned that "classifications . . . based on racial typologies can cause a new divisiveness" and "lead to corrosive discourse" where race serves "as a bargaining chip in the political process" (*Id.*, p. 748). Specifically, Justice Kennedy stated,

> Governmental classifications that command people to march in different directions based on racial typologies can cause new divisiveness. The practice can lead to corrosive discourse, where race serves not as an element of our diverse political heritage but instead as a bargaining chip in the political process. On the other hand race-conscious measures that do not rely on differential

> treatment based on individual classifications present these problems to a lesser degree. (*Id.*, p. 797)

Concerns for hostility are legitimate and must play a part in full examinations of evidence to determine the legitimacy of differential treatment.

The law's concern for group hostility may be well taken, but it also may be misplaced. For example, it assumes that people who experience differential treatment actually care about the cause—people experiencing hostility from someone or an institution may feel that hostility regardless of whether it relates to a governmental policy. In addition, the government policy may not directly call for differential treatment, but the government may create contexts that allow it to flourish, such as in schools or justice systems. Last, the legal system's efforts to create equality, by treating groups the same way, itself may contribute to hostility. Again, these possibilities highlight not only the need for empirical analyses but also a need to take the legal system's proffered rationales seriously and consider them along with other rationales and assumptions.

Avoiding the Loss of Governmental Benefits

Harms that arise from the denial of specific services provide another key reason for not pursuing classifications based on differential treatment. In some instances, some groups will not suffer if one receives differential treatment to enhance its equality, but finding such situations remains difficult. In addition, those are not the only difficulties. Although some costs can be identified for the group that does not receive the benefit, costs do not come alone. Some costs come with benefits, such as when costs to an individual could benefit the group as a whole. The educational context reveals how these concerns can take many forms.

The harm associated with the denial of services emerges in a variety of ways. It is illustrated in the effects of preferential treatment in admissions decisions and the denial of admissions to some individuals. It also arises in the potential costs that integration might have on majority students. For example, majority students may have reduced opportunities and achievement; integration also may create difficult situations for majority students to benefit from what they would otherwise receive from the government. The potential harm also can arise in the costs to society, such as through stereotyping and institutional racism (Halpern et al., 2011). To complicate matters, by denying access to some in the majority group that already had access, those who continue to have access may have different experiences that they would not have otherwise had. Those experiences can be either harmful or beneficial; they even can be both. These issues and concerns run rampant in this area of law, but they again do not provide clear answers as to how much weight should be given to them. Still, they too raise issues open to empirical analysis.

Possible concerns about preferential treatment for one group need not lead to the conclusion that differential treatment is inappropriate. However, resources tend to be limited, costs necessarily factor into the social provision of any service, and costs and benefits are not always clear. If anything, however, the concerns show room for benefitting from empirical analyses. What may appear as a theoretically appropriate and just solution, such as integration, actually may not work out that way in practice. Just as some cures for physical ailments may be more harmful than the ailments, so can some remedies to socially created harms.

Avoiding the Usurpation of Local Powers

The running theme relating to how much weight to give to the costs of differential treatment relates to a final key point: the extent to which communities are entitled to judicial deference. In many instances, courts view local school districts as having great expertise in matters affecting education, therefore entitling them to judicial deference. That expertise also is deemed important for education as a whole because it permits experimentation. The pull of granting schools latitude to experiment for educational excellence is met by the push of needing to ensure basic rights. Both issues of expertise and experimentation invite empirical analyses.

The previously mentioned concerns have been raised in desegregation cases. The Court reveals deference to local school authorities and has emphasized the discretionary authority of local school boards in matters of educational policy setting. But, on the other hand, the Court has been willing to interfere and protect the rights that everyone should enjoy. Notably, in his dissent in *Parents Involved* (2007, p. 855), Justice Breyer found that there were no "reasonably evident alternatives" by which the districts could reach their goals for diversity. More than the other justices, he was willing to defer to the local school boards'

> knowledge, expertise, and concerns in these particular matters . . . since judges are not well suited to act as school administrators . . . [and] local school boards better understand their own communities and have a better knowledge of what in practice will best meet the educational needs of their pupils. (*Id.*, p. 848)

Despite his plea, the majority of his colleagues thought otherwise; they were willing to impose a federal standard on local communities.

Whether the federal courts, let alone the Supreme Court, should intervene and essentially create social policy remains contentious. It is true that the Court always makes social policy with every decision it makes or refuses to make and that the Court cannot avoid doing so. However, interference makes the judiciary an explicit policy-making body and, by doing so, creates partisan divisions. These divisions are expected and deemed problematic in that justices become a group of non-elected "legislators" who seek to decide what kind of society Americans should try to construct. They also are problematic to the extent that the judiciary may lack the institutional capacity to understand thoroughly the relevant local intricacies and variations.

Despite limitations in having a judiciary that essentially crafts social policy, this area of law is fraught with examples of judicial interference deemed necessary to set broadly acceptable standards that respect rights deemed too important to leave to the discretion of local decision makers. In fact, this area of law reveals the hazards of leaving matters to local communities. Sometimes the rights of minorities need to be protected by limiting those of the majority group.

Who is best suited to make policy decisions may be a political matter, but it is also an empirical one. Who is best suited to further governmental goals? Why are they? How can they do so? For example, room for experimentation to reach goals typically is touted for leaving matters to local decision makers. Room for empirical inquiry persists even once that decision is made. It may be that the political decision to give power to one group has been decided, but how that group can use its power effectively again offers several directions for empirical inquiry. Decisions need not be made without a grounding in empirical findings, just as the Court itself submits governmental policies affecting important rights to close scrutiny.

The Call for Caution in Identifying Empirical Needs

The legal system raises many empirical issues when it determines whether and how to make distinctions among groups of individuals, but that does not make the identification of empirical needs an easy task. Many reasons for caution emerge when seeking to address legal issues. Examining empirical issues involves much more, for example, than determining whether the identified compelling interests are being met appropriately. The need for caution arises because the law is far from settled and the questions raised often have multiple reasonable solutions.

The need for caution becomes plain in the different visions of *Brown* articulated in *Parents Involved*. In its move toward adopting a color-blind Constitution, *Parents Involved* has been accused of abandoning *Brown's* core values. However, it remains debatable whether it signals such an abandonment. Arguably, the Court's recent decisions simply abandon *Brown*, particularly in terms of the remedial impulses *Brown* had fostered. Also arguably, on the other hand, the Court merely clarifies *Brown's* core principle of nondiscrimination and suggests a need to change fundamentally the legal system's approach to eliminating educational inequality. That reasonable people could hold either of these views reveals the need for caution: Determinations of when the government can intervene and what it can do remain profoundly undetermined. This need for caution has at least five dimensions relevant to considering the law's empirical needs.

The Arbitrariness of Compelling Interests

The notion of compelling interests itself remains somewhat arbitrary. It is rarely clear when a government interest is "compelling" enough, when an action is justified by a societal need of sufficient magnitude. This lack of clarity is important because the most important question in many constitutional questions involves the manner in which a court characterizes legal arguments in terms of interests that are either compelling or merely legitimate. The same sense of arbitrariness emerges when the Court determines whether governmental interests needed to justify infringing on rights need to be compelling or simply legitimate. The latter issue arises when the Court determines whether rights are fundamental, somewhat important, or neither.

The possibility of arbitrariness in what the law deems compelling raises important concerns. One concern is that the Supreme Court simply follows the political climate of the moment when identifying any particular interest as sufficiently compelling to outweigh the right of individuals to equal treatment. Such reliance raises the concern that empirical formulations may not matter and, equally important, empirical formulations also simply may reflect the political climate rather than science's claimed dispassionate, unbiased, and closer approximation to truth.

Leading cases addressing differential treatment due to racial group status actually are keenly aware of this concern and the dangers it poses. Toward the end of his opinion in *Parents Involved* (2007), Justice Thomas lambasted policies that promote racial integration as the product of "faddish social theories" and cautions us to "beware of elites bearing racial theories" (*Id.*, pp. 780–781):

> Indeed, if our history has taught us anything, it has taught us to beware of elites bearing racial theories. . . . Can we really be sure that the racial theories that motivated *Dred Scott* and *Plessy* are a relic of the past or that future theories will be nothing but beneficent and progressive? That is a gamble I am unwilling to take, and it is one the Constitution does not allow. (*Id.*, pp. 780–782)

Even a rigorous amount of scrutiny may not save the legal system from unsound constitutional results. Research may be helpful, but the empirical record still reveals the need to be wary of policies that may be more arbitrary than they seem. That record even reveals the need to be wary of research that itself may be problematic. The political climate may be difficult to separate from empirical findings, and vice versa.

The Subjective Nature of Cost–Benefit Analyses

The process of identifying empirical needs and relying on research remains arbitrary to the extent that it may or may not yield results consistent with public expectations. This arbitrariness may emerge because the desirability of any social action rests on the perception of both the nature and the allocation of costs and benefits. Regrettably, who should receive the benefits and pay the costs, and even how to make the calculation, remains unclear. Resolutions may involve empirical conclusions, but other factors likely play important roles. This issue particularly arises to the extent that judicial decisions can be subjective.

Subjective balancing of costs and benefits enters determinations of the relative weight of empirical findings. For example, the question regarding the legality of a race-conscious program rests entirely on whether a decision maker finds its probable outcome worth the sacrifice it entails. Rather than producing outcomes objectively consistent with a particular law, outcomes reflect the importance and desirability that particular justices place on an expected consequence of a policy.

The lack of objectivity in the weight given to costs and benefits is revealed, for example, in different justices' views of whether an interest is compelling and what evidence could be used to meet that threshold standard. In *Parents Involved*, all members of the Court found that the use of race in the challenged policies had only minimal effects on students' assignments to schools. The Court interpreted that minimal effect as a lack of necessity for the policy. The minimal effect meant that the plan's goals could be met by other means. The dissenting justices interpreted the minimal effect to mean the opposite, as they argued that minimal effects reflected the assignment plans' appropriately narrow focus and highlighted their need. Their point was well taken in that, as previously seen, the entire concept of narrow tailoring mandates minimal effects. However, they were in the minority. Such disagreements leave constitutional jurisprudence vulnerable to the argument that constitutionality reflects a decision maker's own scheme of values, the type of equality the decision maker deems appropriate to pursue. That leaves empirical analyses in a difficult bind because their utility and relevance vary depending on somewhat subjective judgments.

Legal Rules Lack Finality

The method for determining the government's appropriate role in remedying outcomes also remains essentially underdetermined and does not guide empirical analyses as clearly as one might expect. This area of law is now guided by a simple rule. Under *Parents Involved*, remedies for dealing with racial imbalances in primary and secondary school contexts can come only after the legal system itself caused the racial imbalance. However, this rule is not as clearly settled as it appears; it defies easy analysis.

As much as the Court seeks finality, it often cannot reach it. This area of law is full of instances in which dissenting opinions eventually become adopted by majority views, and vice versa. This is particularly the case in split decisions such as *Parents Involved*. This unsettled aspect of law is due to changes in law as well as the law's adaptation to society. Adaptation to societal needs may reveal room for empirical research, but that research may not resolve disputes.

The role of finality gains significance when courts have supported the use of racial preferences in ways that suggest no limiting principles. This appears particularly true at post-secondary school levels, the context that has most articulated the use of racial classifications in admissions decisions. For example, it is unclear how courts will be able to determine when stigma has been attenuated and by how much it needs to be attenuated. The same is true for racial understanding and the other accepted rationales for supporting racial preferences—demographic parity, classroom diversity, and avoiding racial isolation.

The challenges that come with a lack of finality are worth emphasizing as they relate to the utility of empirical research to guide legal analyses. If evidence is difficult to find, then courts are left with the difficult question of whether, and how much, to defer to government officials. This concern was at the heart of the most recent case involving racial preferences in admissions decisions: *Fisher II* (2016). In that case, the majority and dissent sparred along the lines of deference to university officials. The Supreme Court originally had asked the lower court to engage in a more searching scrutiny, but the appellate court balked and ruled for the university without conducting that analysis. Upon revisiting the case, the Supreme Court accepted the university's good faith efforts, which the dissent rejected on the grounds that such deference insulates affirmative action policies from judicial review.

The Law Need Not Reflect Empirical Reality

The need for caution in identifying empirical needs also emerges because the legal system adopts formalities that need not reflect empirical reality. The law's reliance on legal myths is legendary. The reason for that reliance is that the legal system must make assumptions to resolve disputes; reasonable lines must be drawn even though evidence may support another line. This raises the caution that empirical research may be focusing on one approach to legal issues and ignoring what else could be relevant. It also raises the caution that the law's reliance on legal myths makes empirical research irrelevant.

How the Court currently construes when it will permit remedies in situations such as *Parents Involved* again provides examples of the possibility that the legal system can render empirical research irrelevant or lead researchers to focus on issues that appear relevant but do not really address what individuals experience. The Court permits remedial plans to address the historical use of racial classifications if those plans have been motivated by judicial mandates. However, the inquiry to uncover whether a community ever has been subject to a de jure school desegregation order remains problematic. Arguably, civil rights reform sought change without bringing school systems to court. The goal was to move society toward equality by affecting individuals' hearts and minds, changing how groups interacted, and opening opportunities for individual and societal advancement. The Court in *Brown* set the standard so that schools could follow it en mass. The Court did not do so to invite more litigation. It did so to end litigation. That was, after all, the Court's mandate in *Brown v. Board of Education* (*Brown II*, 1955, p. 301) when it revisited the manner by which states were to implement the principle of nondiscrimination, found that it would need to vary depending on local conditions, and tasked the states to address the issue "with all deliberate speed."

However, the majority of justices on the Supreme Court does not see it that way. *Brown II* (1955, p. 299) gave courts the power to oversee, but it gave responsibility to school authorities: "School authorities have the primary responsibility for elucidating, assessing, and solving these problems; courts will have to consider whether the action of school authorities constitutes good faith implementation of the governing constitutional principles." Giving the judicial system the power to oversee becomes critical. The Court deems school districts that entered into voluntary integration plans for the express reason of staying out of court and avoiding the imposition of a "remedy" as not having acted pursuant to a "remedial" order. The result is that schools that acted prospectively and as hoped to address group disparities in school assignments and opportunities now no longer can do so. The disparities remain outside of possible legal recourse—the government cannot deliberately rebalance them.

Disagreement about school districts' responses to *Brown*—whether they acted because of *Brown* generally or they acted specifically because a court permitted or required them to do so—makes a difference. Rather than examining what was done and why, the legal system can rely on formalized distinctions that determine the nature of motivations. The Court can accept judicially formalized mandates and ignore voluntary actions to avoid judicial decrees of wrongdoing. The upshot is that reliance on formal distinctions plays down the utility of empirical analyses and fails to offer guidance on what the government actually did.

The reliance on formalized distinctions is particularly effective in avoiding empirical analyses. In this instance, the best evidence indicates that the Court in *Parents Involved* was on the wrong side of empirical findings. Reductions in segregation actually were greater in districts that were not under court orders to desegregate (Logan, Oakley, & Stowell, 2008). This is not to say that court orders were not needed. However, although much of the desegregation that happened was voluntary, that voluntariness emerged in response to potential threats of lawsuits as well as aggressive federal enforcement and support that bolstered district leaders' belief in integration's social and educational goal (see also Reardon & Owens, 2014). Individuals and institutions respond to all types of court "orders," not just those resulting from their own litigation.

Social Phenomena Change

The need for caution also emerges because we are dealing with evolving phenomena. The legal system evolves and changes, and so do the issues that it addresses. In this area of law, even the nature of classifications remains problematic. In addition, the nature of what constitutes diversity continues to change. Changes in existing labels and meanings attached to them challenge responses to them.

Even what may appear immutable is subject to alteration, particularly in terms of the meaning attached to it. Racial lines continuously blur, and diversity has become a multifaceted concept composed of biological, ethnic, social, and economic factors. The nature of racial and ethnic diversity evolves drastically to encompass a multiplicity of groups and subgroups of different cultures, traditions, generations, and ethnicities. Indeed, individual identification with racial and ethnic identities changes over the life course, particularly during the adolescent period (Kiang, Witkow, Baldelomar, & Fuligni, 2010). This recognition becomes important in that the significance of change again is undetermined.

The changes can support different arguments. They could support claims that the government should not categorize individuals into arbitrarily defined racial groups for the purposes of differential treatment. They also can support the claim that the legal system may use classifications if society has not made full progress toward true diversity given the very nature of the diverse experiences. They also can challenge race-conscious policies that do not directly use racial classifications. Also problematic is the encouragement of the development of policies to address racially related social problems by moving away from using race as the primary means of classification. This results from the need to avoid the rigidity of a strict scrutiny analysis. The changing nature and significance of race implicates these efforts: Race-conscious policies reach effectiveness only if properly targeted, and efforts to not discriminate based on race need a good sense of what counts as race.

Cautions Are Not Inherently Problematic

The previously discussed reasons for caution may be problematic for the effective use of empirical research, but they need not be so. They allow for flexibility. Although this area of law has become settled at this point in legal developments and use of empirical findings, room for maneuvering remains. As much as current case law appears settled, it is not. What *Brown* said and what happened after it make clear that the law leaves open to interpretation what may seem well established, even when the law results from a unanimous legal decision such as *Brown*. In *Parents Involved*, the justices who limited the use of racial classifications had identified two compelling state interests, but they left open the possibility of recognizing others in the future. By doing so, the Court also opens the door to empirical claims. Considering that the dissenting justices had made some of those empirical claims, it appears that if there is any majority opinion in this area of law, it is that empirical analyses can play decisive roles in the legal system's future. That openness permits different legal responses that call for empirical analyses.

Conclusions

The Constitution's equal protection mandate does not apply to everything that the government does. The government can make distinctions among groups of individuals and treat them differently. It routinely does so. However, its ability to do so is constrained when some of the groups are protected because of a history of invidious treatment by law and society. Those constraints mean that the legal system must determine which group classifications are worthy of heightened protection, the compelling interests that can permit differential treatment, and the effectiveness of policies and other governmental actions that would further the legitimate compelling interests. Those constraints, however, are not always clear. A look at how the legal system addresses constraints relating to racial classifications reveals enduring disputes in the creation of classifications, remedies, and justifications.

The previously mentioned developments profoundly influence the potential relevance and utility of empirical evidence. All approaches to resolving disputes do lend themselves to considerations of empirical formulations and findings. However, caution is warranted when identifying the needed empirical findings. The legal system's approaches often appear more settled than they actually are, both legal responses and empirical findings are subject to problematic biases, the legal system may adopt formalities that challenge the utility of empirical research, and the legal system simply may not reflect reality when it creates classifications. Empirical analyses must, then, scrutinize the needs that the law articulates and the situations that laws address. Importantly, just as the legal system has its own goals, ideals, and ways of doing things, so does empirical research. Part of research's ideals is that some topics are too important to be ignored or addressed without close empirical scrutiny. How society addresses racial segregation and diversity, regardless of its causes and manifestations, is one of those topics.

In other words, both society and the legal system itself demand empirical analyses. Those analyses are needed to evaluate the general rationales supporting the development of legal doctrine. Equally important, they are needed to scrutinize the implementation of the resulting legal rules applied in specific cases. This is so because the law is guided by broad legal rules, developed by their application in specific cases, and legitimized through sound analysis.

4

Empirical Assessments of Legal Doctrine Responding to School Segregation and Diversity

Two Needed Empirical Assessments of the Government's Legitimate Responses

The utility of empirical findings rests on the relevant legal disputes and the interpretive mechanisms that will lead to their resolution. These determinative factors are at play in the legal system's responses to racial/ethnic status. As expected, however, disputes raise complex and challenging concerns. In addition, the legal system itself, including the manner the Court interprets infringements on Constitutional rights, has undergone important transformations since *Brown v. Board of Education* (1954). These developments are not necessarily negative. In fact, they are the opposite. The transformation and enduring disputes leave expanding room for considering empirical findings. Although courts need not turn to empirical evidence, the framework used to determine the nature of the interests at stake and the outcomes of potential legal rules clearly lend themselves to informative empirical analyses.

Determining the legitimacy of the government's classifications of individuals based on their race requires addressing two areas of research. The first area centers on understanding the significance of the government's role in both segregation and desegregation—all narrowly defined along the lines taken by anti-classification approaches to achieve equality. The second area of research considers anti-subordination approaches, which include identifying multiple compelling governmental interests supporting integration efforts, rather than mere desegregation. A close look at empirical findings relating to the legitimacy of governmental actions also must include an interpretative analysis of those findings to think through the findings that we have as well as those that we do not have.

Empirical Assessments of Anti-Classification Approaches

As *Brown* reveals, and as all current Supreme Court justices apparently agree in *Parents Involved in Community Schools v. Seattle School District No. 1* (2007), remedying the effects of past de jure (legally mandated) differential treatment based on race serves as an appropriate compelling interest for using race-conscious policies to remedy the negative effects of that differential treatment. Thus, if governmental action led directly to the inappropriate discrimination, the state may marshal its resources to address the effects of that discrimination. Although some justices espousing the anti-classification approach reject the use of classifications, they remain open, in narrow sets of circumstances, to remedying the inappropriate use of classifications, as long as, for example, the remedies are narrowly tailored and necessary.

As much as the previously mentioned approach receives support from the judiciary, it receives strikingly mixed support from empirical research. The law and empirical research appear at opposite ends in their support of what is now basic doctrine, with even considerable research directly contradicting legal mandates. Available evidence essentially points to two conclusions. Segregation need not be harmful and in fact may be beneficial, but much may depend on the nature and reason for the segregation. Desegregation may not be beneficial; it most likely reaps expected benefits when implemented in ways that consider other factors, such as the socioeconomic status of students and schools. However, desegregation only for desegregation's sake likely is ineffective, and the same is true for segregation. Much depends on the details.

Segregation's Effects

Jurisprudence relating to equal protection may concern itself with the negative effects of the state's role in segregating based on race, but researchers examining segregation's effects generally have not heeded the call to support such claims. Remarkably, researchers have yet to produce systematic and robust research differentiating the effects of segregation due to the legal system's direct intervention. This is not to say that research focusing directly on segregation and desegregation does not exist. However, it is to say that existing research tends not to offer the robust conclusions that might be expected if evaluations must focus on the government's explicit role.

Research presented in *Brown* serves as an appropriate starting point for illustrating the importance of research relating directly to the disputed legal issue, which was the harm of segregation based on race. In *Brown* itself, the empirical research offered in support of segregation's harm actually had little probative force. The evidence's main theme suggested that from a very young age, Black children are sensitive to and strongly affected by prejudice and discrimination generally. That broad trend in findings was not surprising. Being treated badly tends to elicit negative effects.

The trend in findings may make sense, but it failed to address legal issues. None of the empirical studies brought to the Court's attention directly addressed the legal question raised by the case. Nor did oral testimony isolate the effects of public school segregation per se (Gregor, 1963; van den Haag, 1960). The plaintiff's legal brief to the Court similarly did not purport to address public school segregation either. Even the appellant's brief, which was deemed as presenting the relevant scientific findings, actually ignored the issue that was on point. Instead, the presented research referred to a broad statement of race relations and the negative effects of discrimination and prejudice—a statement largely derived from the opinions of social scientists who had expertise in social psychology or race relations (Carter, 1953). The only study that most closely addressed the question on point was an article reporting the undocumented opinions of social scientists in response to a nationwide poll (Deutscher & Chein, 1948). Especially when viewed in light of current standards for conducting research, the study considerably lacked rigor. It may be unfair to judge early research in this area by today's standards, but the research lacked clear relevance, a limitation that may explain why scholars, as well as the justice who wrote the *Brown* opinion, viewed the citation to the empirical evidence as tangential.

If the briefs presenting empirical research did not much focus directly on the issue of segregation's effects on the group being discriminated against, they certainly did not present much direct evidence of segregation's effects on the majority group. The Court chose not to pursue the notion that segregation generated dual harm. It was aware of research relating to dual harms, as the briefs also had contained opinions of the psychological harms for the majority, and thus society as a whole. They presented the conclusion as they emphasized that the effects on the subordinating group were more obscure and subtle. The briefs noted that individuals in the majority group who learn prejudices also are taught to gain personal status in unrealistic and nonadaptive ways. These ways could include feelings of guilt or of hostility and aggression against whole groups of people that they use to protect themselves from recognizing the injustices (Clark, Chein, & Cook, 1952). Although that evidence appeared just as strong as evidence relating to the negative effects on Black youth, the Court did not pursue the notion that the myth of Black inferiority coexisted with the myth of White superiority.

Given *Brown's* ruling, if there was an absence of directly relevant research before it, there likely will never be directly probative research after it. In a literal sense, the negative association of government-endorsed segregation was removed with *Brown* in 1954. As a result, the effects of government-ordered segregation could not be evaluated later. Still, as a practical matter, little desegregation took place during the next decade, which allowed researchers to investigate the effects of segregation. And, it was investigated. These studies are of significance in that they increased in empirical rigor, but they also operated on the assumption that aspirations and self-esteem of segregated students still might reflect what could have been found had the studies been conducted prior to the Court's desegregation decision. The assumption may be a large one, but the studies still center on the law's role in segregating, which certainly increases their relevance.

Direct Research on Segregation's Effects

Research examining segregation's effects appropriately centered on educational and occupational aspirations as well as self-esteem. Reviews of research relating to aspirations have reported consistent findings (Epps, 1975; Proahansky & Newton, 1968; Weinberg, 1977). Among the most notable findings were those that compared the aspirations of Blacks to those of Whites. Across the board, the studies found that the level of aspirations of segregated Blacks was as high or higher than that of segregated Whites. These were striking findings and somewhat unexpected given the rationales supporting *Brown*. Importantly, studies examining self-esteem also found results contrary than expected when comparing the self-esteem of Blacks with that of Whites. Reviews have found that the self-concept of segregated Blacks was either favorable or better than that of Whites (Epps, 1975, Rosenberg & Simmons, 1972; Stephan, 1978; Weinberg, 1977; Zirkel, 1971). Importantly, research did identify some potential nuances, such that there may be variation based on age, with those of younger Black children being lower than those of White children (Stephan, 1978). Also, these general trends reflect current ones—annual surveys reveal that African American adolescents have higher self-esteem than any other ethnic group in the United States (Bachman, O'Malley, Freedman-Doan, Trzesniewski, & Donnellan, 2011), and reviews of the literature reveal that their advantage increases as they go through adolescence (Gray-Little & Hafdahl, 2000). Still, the general findings were strikingly consistent and in the opposite direction of what likely was expected after *Brown* as well as even today.

The consistency of findings pointing in unexpected directions poses important problems for those who would have legal systems follow empirical findings. The findings may be difficult to interpret, but researchers have provided suggestions. It could be that there was a change in Black self-esteem due to, for example, changes in civil rights. Yet another possibility relates to methodological matters, with indirect measures (dolls, toys, and drawings) being replaced with self-report questionnaires and rating scales, with earlier research using more indirect techniques. A related difficulty in interpreting the findings involves the assumptions relating to the measures used and the validity of inferences drawn from methodologies used, such as whether an ethnic preference (Black children choosing Black dolls to play with) relates to personal self-esteem and whether self-reports actually reflect reality. The general point that can be made about research in this area is that it no longer is possible to support or even discount the assertion that government-enforced segregation lowers the self-esteem and educational aspirations of children. In fact, it may well not be able to be supported today despite showings of racial/ethnic disparities in schooling.

Indirect Research on Segregation's Effects

Given that segregation officially ended with the Supreme Court's decision to abolish it, researchers face important challenges in efforts to study the effects of government-endorsed segregation. As a result and just as with *Brown*, some of the most relevant research examining the effects of segregation due to legal mandates still comes from experimental research relating to the effects of widespread but unfounded beliefs about racial inferiority on the academic performance of minority students. The phenomenon, best known as "stereotype threat," reveals how beliefs about inferiority undermine performance.

Stereotype threat works in a predictable manner. Students perceiving stereotypic expectations about their own intellect from teachers and fellow students and who are motivated to disprove these stereotypes can become distracted in stressful assessment situations, such as testing, and fail to perform to their capacity (Steele & Aronson, 1995). Although much of the empirical research documenting the effects of stereotype threat has been conducted with college students, research also indicates that stereotype threat can affect elementary school-aged children. In addition to negatively affecting short-term academic achievement scores, stereotype threat may lead students to adopt habits that undermine future academic success (Alexander & Schofield, 2006). Still, even if researchers could grant that this area of research presents compelling findings, the findings again do not address directly the legal issue at hand.

Conclusions from Segregation Research

The state of the evidence leads to at least three conclusions. First, the lack of findings, but especially those that contradict the general beliefs regarding segregation's effects on self-esteem, poses significant problems for a legal system that would take empirical research seriously. Identifying a compelling state interest based on the available research, rather than doctrine, certainly leads to conclusions that conflict with broad societal values and ideals. Second, there may not be a need to demonstrate negative effects because they may be assumed and deemed a matter of common sense. This was the position suggested by leading legal commentators at the time (Black, 1960; Wechsler, 1959) who did not find the Court's use of social science persuasive and, for that matter, did not find the Court's legal rationales for its conclusions that persuasive either. Third, rather than focus on segregation, attention can turn to the effects of desegregation. If it could be shown that legal intervention leads to positive outcomes, then grounds may exist for showing that the segregation in the first instance was, if not harmful, then at least problematic. This may be an odd way to demonstrate the law's effect, but it may well remain necessary given the challenges of addressing segregation in the first instance. It also may be necessary given that current jurisprudence would seem to require a reasonable demonstration of harm.

Desegregation's Effects

Unlike a pervasive lack of research that would be directly on point relating to segregation, literally hundreds of investigations have examined the effects of the legal system's desegregation efforts aimed to redress the law's segregation based on race. That research typically has examined the key outcomes of perennial interest since *Brown*: the effects of desegregation on student achievement, self-esteem, and intergroup relationships. Legally, these outcomes are of significance because removing the burden of segregation should result in positive outcomes. These three outcomes also are worth focusing on given that they have garnered the best research in this area, that the research has been the subject of important reviews (Epps, 1981; Longshore & Prager, 1985; St. John, 1975; Stephan, 1978), and that the research remains illustrative of other findings and their implications. Still, research on desegregation's effects may fill volume after volume, but that abundance of findings has not yielded results that readily support desegregation's expected benefits.

The general conclusion that emerges from this area of research is that findings reveal weak and inconsistent effects and generally view desegregated schooling neither as a demonstrated success nor as a demonstrated failure. Indeed, some major literature reviews of the research on desegregation's effects find studies' methodological limitations to be so problematic as to question the studies' legitimacy and relative worth (Bradley & Bradley, 1977; St. John, 1975). These are strong conclusions. Regardless of whether such strong cautions are on target, as examined later, the research still remains important to consider. Taken together, the studies shed light on important issues and nuances to consider in efforts to lay the empirical foundation for broad social efforts seeking to restructure relationships based on race.

Self-Esteem Effects

Given the concern that segregation led to reduced self-esteem, it is not surprising that research has examined the relationship between desegregation and self-esteem. The general rule that emerges from reviews of findings in this area is that wide inconsistencies make it difficult to discern an overall pattern and draw an overall conclusion. For example, one review of studies reports that desegregation actually may have harmed minority youth's self-esteem, especially academic self-esteem (St. John, 1975). Another review reports unfavorable effects (Weinberg, 1977). Another concludes that the self-esteem of Blacks rarely increased in desegregated schools (Stephan, 1978). Others conclude by avoiding generalizations (Epps, 1978, 1981). In terms of the effects of desegregation on Black youth's self-esteem, then, the evidence fails to support a clear benefit. Here, it is important to emphasize again that the research focused on desegregation, not general group differences that generally reveal Black youth as having the highest self-esteem.

Race Relations Effects

Research relating to the effects of segregation research also has focused on race relations, given that a major legal rationale supporting desegregation rested on the claim that it would improve race relations. However, like research relating to self-esteem, research on intergroup relationships does not support a general conclusion on the effect of desegregation (see reviews by Schofield, 1978; St. John, 1975; Stephan, 1978). For example, one review examined 24 studies, with only 2 of them dealing solely with nonvoluntary desegregation, involving interracial schooling in the period of 1968–1974. The review found mixed results for interracial acceptance and attitudes (Cohen, 1975; similar to St. John, 1975). Another reviewer examined the effects of planned school desegregation, since 1960, on attitudes and concluded that methodological problems rendered them all uninterpretable (McConahay, 1978). Another review concluded that if a general conclusion can be deduced, then it likely is that desegregation leads to increases in Black prejudices toward Whites as frequently as it leads to decreases, and White's prejudices toward Blacks tends to increase somewhat more frequently than decrease (Stephan, 1978). Yet another review of 39 studies of schools that had undergone planned desegregation concluded that the findings showed positive attitudes among Blacks and/or Whites (Weinberg, 1977). These often conflicting conclusions of reviews of similar (and sometimes the same) studies reveal that the type of desegregation matters and that desegregating, per se, need not result in the positive intergroup relationships that might be expected to result from the legal mandate that segregation needed to end in order, partly, to improve race relations.

Achievement Effects

Research relating to self-esteem and race relations may not lead to clear outcomes, but that is less the case for reviews of studies of desegregation's effect on achievement. Generally, these reviews reveal that desegregation results in more positive than negative effects on minority students' achievement (Crain & Mahard, 1978; Schofield, 1995). The findings also reveal no effect on White achievement, although the research base for this conclusion remains meager (Schofield, 1995).

Despite the positive findings, achievement can involve a variety of outcomes, and not surprisingly, the effects of desegregation on achievement can vary depending on the outcomes measured. Thus, research examining the academic effects of desegregation reveals a positive impact on reading achievement but little or no effect on math scores (Armor, 1984; Miller & Carlson, 1984; Wortman, 1984). The findings also may vary depending on the minority group under study. Thus, although findings relating to Latino students' achievement are more limited, a review of the literature on the effect of school desegregation found that those studies reported modestly positive or no effect on Latino achievement (Horn & Kurlaender, 2006; Schofield, 1995). Given these factors that can produce important variations in findings, some reviews expectedly report mixed results. For example, some find the results inconsistent and argue that they provide no assurance that desegregation will confer achievement gains (Bradley & Bradley, 1977; St. John, 1975), and some report that two-thirds of reviewed studies (out of 34) reveal no positive effects. Still, studies that focus on planned desegregation (omitting studies of other mixed-race schools) reveal positive effects, with one analysis of 49 studies reporting that 60 percent resulted in achievement gains for Blacks (Weinberg, 1975, 1977) and another analysis of 73 studies finding positive effects in half to two-thirds of the cases (Crain & Mahard, 1978). Even the most positive spins on research relating to achievement, then, still report a pervasive lack of effects.

Rather than focusing on achievement in certain academic areas, some studies have centered on graduation rates. Analyses of national census data that have examined the effects of desegregation on dropout rates (Guryan, 2004) have found that desegregation plans of the 1970s linked to significant declines in Black high school students' dropout rates during the decade; they also have shown that districts that had not initiated desegregation efforts had dropout rates that remained constant. In addition, the studies showed that the effects were especially strong in districts that practiced mandatory desegregation and also those that reduced within-school segregation from tracking (Guryan, 2004). They also revealed that White students' dropout rates were not affected, which included the finding that they did not decline (Guryan, 2004). Other studies reported similar results. A three-decade study of high school dropping out in Cleveland revealed that under segregation, both Whites and minorities dropout rates suffered. Desegregation linked to better rates for all groups. Importantly, however, the study reported that even though school desegregation linked to favorable effects on students' graduation rates, other adverse social forces in students' urban environments were strong countervailing forces (Saatcioglu, 2010). Some studies have found that attending a high socioeconomic status school may have a disparate effect on different minority groups' dropout rates, with Asian youth typically having reduced dropout rates but Mexican youth having an increased likelihood of dropout (Saatcioglu, 2010). Variations in the strength of these relationships may exist, as continued to be revealed by many studies published in the current decade (Reardon & Owens, 2014).

The empirical record, then, reveals a negative relationship between attending a racially segregated school, particularly high-poverty ones, and the reduced likelihood of graduating from high school. Although some groups may not benefit from high socioeconomic status schools, the rates of graduation tend to increase as youth from all racial and socioeconomic status backgrounds benefit from attending racially diverse schools.

The previous findings relating to achievement find support in meta-analyses that statistically analyze results from numerous students. These analyses, despite individual studies' limitations, reveal important findings that can explain large variations in the results of individual studies. The analyses reported by Crain and Mahard (1978, 1983) are illustrative. First, by sorting studies by their methodological quality, they found that better research on minority achievement tends to result in identifying positive effects. This finding simply may reflect, however, research that was conducted more recently and thus conducted in a different environment than earlier studies. Second, desegregation in the earliest grades results in the most enhancement of Black students' achievement. This finding, in many ways, also would not be surprising in that early interventions tend to be more effective than later ones. Third, desegregation plans with a metropolitan scope show greater Black achievement gains. Arguably, this finding could reflect many other factors at work, such that metro plans reach more middle-class Whites, which makes desegregation socioeconomic as well as racial, or such that metro plans assign more Blacks to high-quality suburban schools. Last, Black students' achievement improves most when Blacks are in schools that are mostly White, another finding that may be attributable to the increased socioeconomic mix in such schools. These types of studies not only show, then, that important nuances exist but also that contextual features of desegregated schools can enhance achievement. They also tend to show that school desegregation can be viewed as resulting in a modest positive effect on the achievement of African American students (Cook, 1984; Crain & Mahard, 1983; Schofield, 1995).

Empirical Assessments of Anti-subordination Approaches

Justices hold different views of compelling interests that would suffice to support the use of anti-subordination approaches to creating race-conscious policies, the interests that would support classifications based on race to achieve racial equality. Some justices identify only a narrow set of potentially compelling interests, whereas others remain open to a broader set of rationales that could support a state's compelling interest in using race-conscious policies. Most notably, however, those adopting anti-subordinating stances are more likely to permit race-conscious policies to address de facto segregation, which involves situations that do not make use of government-imposed racial classifications or that do not result from a larger system of legal apartheid. As with anti-classification approaches, research in this area reveals mixed results. Given that these studies investigate conditions since segregation, the body of reach tends to be more developed and robust. However, in many ways, it also remains limited because it needs to overcome hurdles relating to its relevance.

Diversifying Student Bodies

The government's interest in a diverse student body underpins many of the arguments relating to classifications based on race. That interest, however, can involve multiple dimensions, two of which are important to consider. The first form of interest in a diverse student body can be described as concern about having environments that support "viewpoint diversity." Such diversity is viewed as an interest in having an expansive environment for the exercise and development of free thought that would result from a diverse student body's ability to present diversity in points of view. The second form of interest in a diverse student body relates to the harms associated with racial isolation. The racial isolation argument views diversity in student enrollments as needed to reduce or eliminate the harms of racial isolation in schools (and outside of them). Research speaks to these two interests, but the legal system again sets parameters for determining the type of evidence that matters to support efforts to address those interests.

Enhancing Viewpoint Diversity

At the university level, the Supreme Court has accepted the rationale that enhancing viewpoint diversity can serve as a compelling interest to support race-conscious policies. For example, Justice Powell's *Bakke* decision championed the view that diversity would contribute to the robust exchange of ideas (*Regents of the University of California v. Bakke*, 1978). Links to the diversity of adult's free speech in the university or professional context, however, need not translate to primary or secondary educational levels. In the context of minors' schooling, the interest's relevance remains an open question. Although the argument may face important hurdles, it potentially still offers important insights into the nature of diversity as it applies to adolescents and how that diversity can be both needed and fostered. A close look at the argument in the context of primary and secondary schools also allows for a twist in the legal argument in that the benefits of viewpoint diversity may relate more to academic outcomes than to enhancing critical thinking skills deemed important for effective participation in a democratic society's marketplace of ideas. Thus, the interest may remain, but it could take different forms that may require reformulating the nature and need for the interest.

A first hurdle that the viewpoint diversity rationale must overcome relates to what type of speech and thought warrants support in the context of primary and secondary schools. Without doubt, as the Court itself has noted, these institutions retain the power to inculcate youth and shape their development in ways that are much more controlling and controlled than at university levels. This control is particularly true for free speech because the free speech rights of non-adult students remain severely curtailed. On the other hand, secondary and primary schools dedicate themselves to instilling values of tolerance and preparation for engaging in a democratic society, which includes the protection of diverse views (*Tinker v. Des Moines Independent Community School District*, 1969). Still, whether schools need to respect different views and whether they need to create environments contributing to the development of different views remains an open and complex question. Despite these complexities, empirical studies do provide relevant findings relating to the ability of schools to further those interests (Levesque, 2002).

A second hurdle faced by the viewpoint diversity argument relates to its limits when placed into practice. At its core, the rationale runs the danger of essentializing race in that it rests on the assumption that a person of a given race will have given experiences, express given viewpoints, or contain given ideas. Of course, lack of diversity decreases the likelihood that schools can achieve those goals. Thus, diversity may be a necessary but not sufficient factor to gain exposure to a wide range of people, experiences, and ideas or to achieve a robust exchange of ideas. As detailed later, research suggests that there may be percentage effects (relating to the number of minority students needed for increasing the chances of exchanging diverse ideas) and that much would depend on a particular school's social and academic climate. Still, available research suggests that the diversity of students going into a school or classroom does not ensure a multiplicity of ideas in it, nor does it ensure the expression of diverse viewpoints, let alone their engagement in a manner that results in desired effects.

Placing aside the risks associated with creating situations that essentialize race, both theory and empirical research indicate that learning in diverse classrooms, in arenas permitting students from different backgrounds to communicate their different experiences and perspectives, can result in having students think in more complex ways because it allows them to enhance critical thinking skills and fosters their ability to learn and process knowledge. Two critical factors explain this effect. First, students of different races and ethnic backgrounds actually often do bring different cultural knowledge and social perspectives into their classrooms and, as a result, discussions and interactions with racially diverse groups of students are more likely to enhance critical thinking as they expose students to new information and understandings. Second, that enhancement emerges from appropriately structured learning environments that permit interactions conducive to exchanges that ensure equal status, emphasize cooperation, and provide support from relevant authorities. These general findings, however, have important nuances, with the key one relating to the level of education.

The strongest research supporting the influence of diversity on critical thinking is that on higher education. This area of research has well established that racially and ethnically diverse learning communities link to engagement in active thinking processes, growth in intellectual engagement and motivation, and growth in intellectual and academic skills (Antonio et al., 2004). Meta-analyses confirm that several types of diversity experiences positively relate to several cognitive outcomes (Bowman, 2010). Importantly, those studies also indicate that the magnitude of the effect varies substantially depending on the type of diversity experience, the type of cognitive outcome measured, and the study design (Bowman, 2010). Such complexities are not surprising given that diversity, in and of itself, is insufficient to result in either positive or negative outcomes. The hoped for outcomes emerge when studies closely consider factors that are important in shaping cognitive development, such as the school climate, as confirmed by research examining the general secondary school context (Reyes, Brackett, Rivers, White, & Salovey, 2012) and research particularly relating to racial identity and the school's racial climate (Byrd & Tabbye, 2011). These types of findings importantly reveal the significance of coupling diversity with appropriately structured and supportive policies. They indicate that achieving desired outcomes means more than simply considering diversity in enrollments.

Importantly, claims about enhanced cognitive abilities through diversity at the college level have not been examined as much as those relating to the lower grade levels. Research that does examine those grades tends to substantiate the general findings (Tam & Bassett, 2004). However, research in these contexts tends to focus on academic achievement and outcomes. This important limitation highlights how academic outcomes and achievement in lower grades do not mean what they might at the post-secondary level. Academic outcomes at lower grade levels may not reflect an ability to engage different ideas and accept different viewpoints; instead, they may reflect engagement in orthodoxy. In fact, the ideal of being able to engage materials at a higher level may remain just that, an ideal, even at post-secondary levels.

Still, research focusing on academic outcomes remains instructive. Recent studies untangle the two major dimensions of school racial/ethnic composition—racial/ethnic diversity of the student body and racial/ethnic matching between children and their peers—and determine their relationship to academic development. One study, for example, examined the transition into elementary school and found that school racial/ethnic composition was associated more strongly with children's academic outcomes (Benner & Crosnoe, 2011). That study found that students had higher achievement test scores in more diverse schools and, importantly, that the effect was strongest when students also had more same-race/ethnicity peers in these diverse schools and that these patterns were particularly strong for White students. The diversity interest in the form of students' exposure to a wide range of ideas, backgrounds, and perspectives, then, does appear to extend to kindergarten through 12th grade (K–12) schools, but how it does so remains disputable.

Reducing Racial Isolation

The legal argument supporting diversity in student bodies can rest partly on the contention that diverse student enrollments in schools reduce racial isolation. A school's racial and ethnic diversity shapes cross-race friendship patterns. Using national data on friendship choices from a random sample of students in 7th through 12th grades, an illustrative study examined the effects of an ethnic group's relative size on intergroup friendship choices in schools with varying degrees of racial diversity (Quillian & Campbell, 2003). The study reported that students' racial and ethnic background, in conjunction with a school's racial and ethnic mix, influences the composition of adolescents' friendship networks. It reported that the relative size of an ethnic group in a particular school also influences friendship choices. Moreover, these patterns differed for Whites, Blacks, Asians, and Latinos/as' cross-ethnic friendship choices. Although cross-ethnic friendships that include Asian and Latino/a are more common than those among Blacks and Whites, the likelihood of all cross-ethnic friendships increases with school racial and ethnic diversity. The likelihood that students select friends from their own ethnic group intensifies if they are members of a relatively small minority in a school (less than 10 percent of the school population) (a finding also reported by Feld & Carter, 1998). The authors suggest that growing the ethnic and racial diversity of student populations will lead to notable increases in cross-race friendships only if the national growth in student diversity translates into increasing racial diversity within schools.

Although racial isolation can be reduced at lower educational levels, that reduction gains special significance if it continues into later life. Both theory and evidence suggest that early isolation links to later isolation and that reduced early isolation reduces later isolation. For example, an important study combined data from the US Census with survey data from a large, nationally representative sample of high school students to examine the intersection of high school racial composition and residential neighborhood integration during early adulthood (Goldsmith, 2010). The study found that the proportion of White students in individuals' high schools and later, in their colleges, strongly influences the percentage of White people residing in their adult neighborhoods. Other research has shown that the effects of racial composition of high schools even relate to the racial composition of adults' workplace (Stearns, 2010). Students' exposure to other racial groups in high school—specifically, exposure to Asian American, Latino, and African American students for White students and exposure to Latinos and Whites for African American students—reduces their racial isolation in workplace settings after high school. Remarkably, these effects are detected net of measures of region, high school resources, and individual resources, and particularly net of residential isolation in the neighborhoods that the students lived in during the survey period. These studies are illustrative of those that highlight the long-term effects of attending segregated schools across multiple social settings—racial isolation begets racial isolation.

Critically, the effect of reduced isolation gains significance for what supports it: reduced negative stereotypes and increased tolerance. Social psychologists have demonstrated that intergroup contact mitigates and transforms racial hostility, fear, and stereotypes; conversely, racial isolation tends to perpetuate these racial fears across generations (for a review, see Schofield & Eurich-Fulcer, 2002). An authoritative meta-analysis of more than 500 prior studies that collectively included 250,000 participants showed that greater levels of contact among different groups typically associate with lower levels of intergroup prejudice and that these effects are consistent and significant for samples of children, adolescents, and adults (Pettigrew & Tropp, 2006). Although optimal intergroup conditions—such as equal status between groups, support of institutional authorities, common goals, and cooperation—are not always necessary for reducing prejudice, having those conditions persist leads to larger reductions in prejudice. A related analysis of 198 independent samples from these studies showed that significant, positive effects of intergroup contact typically emerge for samples of children and adolescents in schools and specifically when the contact involves youth from different racial and ethnic groups (Pettigrew & Tropp, 2008). Research appears to have identified important benefits of structured contact among diverse groups.

Research reporting that intergroup contact between groups of unequal status may exacerbate feelings of frustration and prejudice finds parallels in research indicating that the same imbalance may contribute to violence. Graham (2006) found that self-reported victimization was higher in contexts with less ethnic diversity, suggesting that youth tend to be targeted more frequently for victimization in contexts of obvious imbalances in the racial/ethnic composition of classrooms or schools. Other researchers have found that minority students attending racially segregated schools are exposed to more social disorder and violence compared to either Whites or minorities who attend integrated schools (Massey, 2006). Other studies have gone even further and found that attending racially inclusive schools reduces the risk of involvement in the criminal justice system. Blacks attending schools with higher proportions of Whites reduces the likelihood of ending up in prison, but there is no effect for White incarceration rates (LaFree & Arum, 2006). However, research does not always point in the same direction. Some studies report that Black youth attending racially integrated schools are exposed to higher levels of school violence compared to peers attending segregated schools (Eitle & Eitle, 2003). Other studies report that schools with roughly equal ethnic group sizes foster more victimization for White children, less for African American children, and have no effect on the victimization rates of Hispanic children (Hanish & Guerra, 2000). Other studies still find minority students who are in the numerical minority at increased risk for victimization, but that risk depends on the schools' interethnic climate (Agirdag, Demanet, Van Houtte, & Van Avermaet, 2011). Ethnic and racial integration need not lead to improved group relationships.

The potential for highly negative effects of diversity contributes to a growing area of research that seeks to understand the mechanisms that lead to positive outcomes. Research convincingly reveals that the manner in which schools foster contact between youth from different racial and ethnic backgrounds relates to reductions in prejudice and in negative intergroup attitudes (Tropp & Prenovost, 2008). These lines of research reflect the general premises of contact theory's foundations as presented by Allport's (1954) classic work, *The Nature of Prejudice*, which focused on conditions that reduce prejudice. In brief, Allport found that prejudice declined when individuals from different ethnic and racial groups worked together on common goals; shared equal status in situations; worked cooperatively; and were sanctioned by authorities, the law, or by custom. Also, the absence of these conditions resulted in negative effects, leading to the conclusion that intergroup contact can have both alleviating and exacerbating effects on the nature of individuals' intergroup relationships.

The positive outcomes that emerge from diverse school experiences can have long-term effects. These links are understandable through a leading theory in this area of study—perpetuation theory. Perpetuation theory essentially predicts that experiences in racially segregated or integrated schools will affect levels of segregation in students' future social environments on the grounds that differential levels of racial isolation relate to the intergenerational transmission of racial stereotypes, fears, and hostilities. For example, a series of studies found that students from all racial backgrounds who attend diverse secondary schools are more likely to prefer to work and live in diverse settings as adults (Kurlaender & Yun, 2001, 2005, 2007). Other studies reveal that those intentions tend to become reality—that students from integrated schools are more likely to live and work in integrated settings as adults, just as youth from segregated schools likely prefer same-race neighbors (Braddock & Gonzales, 2010, Stearns, 2010, Wells, Holmes, Revilla, & Atanda, 2009). Similarly, a robust study examining the influence of pre-college experiences with cross-racial friendships on the proportion of college cross-raced friendships found that interracial friendships prior to college had the largest impact on the existence of interracial friendships during the first year of college (Stearns, Buchmann, & Bonneau, 2009). The finding was strongest for Whites, who formed more interracial friendships than other groups. Importantly, interracial friendship formation also was influenced by the college environment, such as roommates, ethnic organizations, and Greek organizations. Thus, both positive and negative effects can continue, and whether they do so can depend on the facilitative nature of the contexts in which youth find themselves.

Although perpetuation theory may suggest that integrated schools will result in later life experiences that also are integrated, the link is not that direct. Racial isolation actually can thrive in integrated contexts. We already have seen that the manner in which schools handle racial isolation has important effects on whether it will continue, and those same ways of addressing isolation have an effect on whether they will influence dispositions toward different racial and ethnic groups. In addition, a diverse student body does not necessarily address racial isolation, be it social or otherwise. Studies indicate stronger tendencies for racial homophily in schools with academic tracking. Research on tracking reveals, for example, that tracking can lead to placing White and Asian students into more advanced classes and Black and Latino students into lower-level classes, regardless of ability, which limits the intergroup contact. Although intergroup friendships can occur in these circumstances, they are less likely, as highlighted by commentators viewing these types of efforts as second-generation segregation (Mickelson, 2001; Welner, 2001). On its own, increasing a school's racial diversity does not necessarily lead to reduced isolation. Increasing the number of minority students in schools actually can increase the chances that they will become isolated rather than integrated into other groups. Much depends on how schools structure interactions among students as well as the overall school climate and even the nature of the diversity itself.

Although the different ways that schools can structure relationships retains significance, it remains important to highlight that several of the identified positive effects accrue regardless of whether participants voluntarily choose to engage in intergroup contact. The macro-level studies linking diverse school attendance to diverse neighborhood and work situations provide a strong case in point. Also illustrative are large-scale, longitudinal studies of schooling that focus on the effects of the pre-college interracial interaction experiences of college students. Research has extended the well-established links between meaningful interracial interactions during college to educational and societal benefits (Gurin, Dey, Hurtado, & Gurin, 2002) to pre-college experiences. The most robust and recent study to do so reported the results from a 4-year longitudinal sample of 3,098 undergraduates from 28 colleges and universities (Bowman & Denson, 2012). That study indicated that regardless of the type of outcome and type of pre-college diversity measure, the relationships between college interracial interactions and various outcomes (college satisfaction, emotional well-being, and race-related perceptions) were stronger among students who had had greater pre-college exposure to racial/ethnic diversity. Collectively, findings in this area suggest that contact among youth from different racial groups promotes positive intergroup attitudes, and such positive outcomes become stronger when optimal intergroup conditions are established in the school environment.

Research on racial isolation reveals several important points. First, students learn more than academic lessons in school. Educators, parents, and policymakers expect public schools to prepare students for their lives after high school, in which they will be workers in a globalizing economy and citizens in a multiethnic democratic society. Reducing interracial fears, hostilities, and stereotypes and fostering cross-racial understanding, although insufficient by themselves for achieving public schools' mandates, are important components of children's socialization. Second, even desegregated schools may not foster the intended benefits that come from reducing racial isolation. Allport (1954) identified the optimal conditions for reducing interracial prejudice and fears: cooperative interactions among diverse people with equal status in the social context; shared goals; and support of authorities, law, or custom. Even diverse schools may not have these conditions because the widespread practices of tracking and ability grouping tend to resegregate students at the classroom level. Tracking undermines the potential of school-level diversity to influence, in a positive manner, both achievement and intergroup relationships. Last, integrated schooling may have an impact on cross-racial friendships, including the racial composition of neighborhoods in which individuals live. As discussed previously, researchers have shown that interracial contact can lower levels of stereotypes and prejudice in adult samples. These dispositions transfer to actual relationships, but social structures may influence their fruition.

Enhancing Educational Opportunities

The vast literature on the topic of educational attainment includes several areas of research relevant to understanding schools' ethnic/racial composition effects on students' educational outcomes. At least four areas of study directly relate to educational opportunities in this context: academic achievement in a variety of areas of study, graduation rates, post-secondary educational enrollment, and achievement in post-secondary education. Other areas of study relevant to educational opportunities likely exist, but these four related topics have received the most focus and provide a good sense of research findings relating to the effects of schools' racial/ethnic compositions. Overall, but with important exceptions, research reveals that a school's ethnic/racial composition constitutes an essential component of the opportunity structure that fosters educational opportunities.

Graduation and Dropout Effects

Graduation rates relate to multiple social and individual factors, such as socioeconomic status, family strain, adolescents' risk-taking and commitment to education, as well as neighborhood and school resources. However, a small body of research reveals that the racial composition of schools significantly predicts high school graduation rates. Reviews of early social science literature revealed that attending desegregated elementary and secondary schools decreases the likelihood that minorities will drop out of school (Schofield, 2001). The findings also have been shown for White students, revealing that those who attend predominantly Black or Hispanic high schools are more likely to drop out compared with those who attend integrated or predominantly White schools (Mayer, 1991), a result that relates to findings indicating that attending a high poverty school increased the likelihood of dropping out for all students, especially for low-socioeconomic status students (Mayer, 1991). These types of findings relate to those that focus directly on desegregation and segregation effects. As discussed previously, those studies tend to reveal a negative relationship between attending a racially segregated school, particularly high-poverty ones, and the reduced likelihood of graduating from high school; they also tend to reveal the importance of other factors, such as social forces in students' urban environments (Guryan, 2004; Saatcioglu, 2010). Still, research on school dropout rates remains quite consistent in showing the importance of schools' ethnic and racial compositions.

Academic Achievement

Arguably the most dramatic research findings relating to the effects of integrated schooling address its effects on academic outcomes. These findings are dramatic in that modern studies reveal significant positive effects, whereas early studies pervasively did not. Emblematic of the switch is research that reanalyzed James Coleman et al.'s classic and highly influential 1966 study, *Equality of Educational Opportunity*. The reanalysis revealed opposite effects. Using statistical techniques not available to Coleman and colleagues, recent analyses challenge the widely accepted conclusion that schools are far less important than families for students' academic performance. The analyses find that schools actually are more influential than families and that racial segregation has significant negative effects on achievement (Borman & Dowling, 2010). The new analyses reveal that attending a high-poverty school or a highly segregated African American school has a profound effect on students' achievement outcomes, above and beyond the effect of individual poverty or minority status. Specifically, both the racial/ethnic and social class composition of a student's school are 1¾ times more important than a student's individual race/ethnicity or social class for understanding educational outcomes. These studies may reveal the importance of schools, but the focus on school ethnic/racial composition remains intertwined with school resources themselves, as illustrated by the continued importance of schools' socioeconomic status effects.

The importance of a school's socioeconomic influences cannot be underestimated. Some studies continue to find that although racial segregation matters, schools' socioeconomic compositions rather than racial compositions have the greatest effect on student achievement. For example, one leading longitudinal study investigated achievement growth between grades 8 and 12 in mathematics, science, reading, and history for a large representative sample of students in US high schools (Rumberger & Palardy, 2005). Their model disentangled schools' racial composition and socioeconomic composition effects and found schools' socioeconomic status more important than other factors (see also Borman & Dowling, 2010). These studies highlight the importance of distinguishing the effects of a school's socioeconomic composition from other effects and how the statistical limitations of prior studies may have contributed to erroneous conclusions.

Studies have sought to tease out confounding effects, such as a school's relative socioeconomic status, and have shown increasingly consistent findings. One longitudinal study of four nationally representative databases that spanned a 40-year period examined associations between the Black–White and Latino/a–White test score gaps and changes in schools' minority composition (Berends & Penaloza, 2010). After controlling for other school-level factors and individual and family background measures, increases in school segregation (between 1974 and 2004) corresponded to significant increases in the Black–White and Latino/a–White test score gaps, outweighing the positive changes in family background measures for these minority groups. Another nationally representative sample of high school seniors investigated 5-year predictors of both high school mathematics growth scores and the number and level of math courses (Newton, 2010). The study distinguished the effects of school racial isolation on math outcomes from the effects of other school characteristics, such as socioeconomic composition, and a number of individual-level factors. School composition, defined as percent minority, exerted an adverse effect on both individual math gain scores from 7th through 12th grade and the number and difficulty of math courses completed by high school students. Holding other factors constant, the higher the percent minority in a high school, the lower the students' gains in mathematics achievement and the fewer math courses taken by students. Another study focused on the effects of a state's (Florida) schools' racial composition on achievement outcomes (Borman et al., 2004). After controlling for many school quality, demographic, and family background factors, the authors found that racial isolation has a negative effect on a school's mean on the state's pass rates on comprehensive assessment tests (for reading and mathematics). They concluded that increases in the concentration of Black students in a school related to decreases in the school's mean comprehensive test scores in both reading and mathematics. Last, a meta-analytic study revealed that school racial isolation produces a small but still statistically significant negative effect on overall student mathematics outcomes for the schools (Mickelson, Bottia, & Lambert, 2013). The study found the effects stronger in secondary compared to elementary grades, with racial gaps widening as students aged. This area of research reveals that race gaps due to racial segregation compound over time.

The findings of recent studies of integrated schools are consistent with earlier findings, some of which formally focused on segregation (although not necessarily in the technical sense of the term) (Borman et al., 2004; Caldas & Bankston, 1998). For example, one earlier study using National Assessment of Educational Progress data across every state found that controlling for socioeconomic status eliminates most of the negative relationship with segregated schools and achievement only for White students but not for

Black students; however, it also concluded that the relationship varied among states (Armor, 2006). Another study found that a decrease in the percentage of Black classmates for Black students, particularly when cumulated over many years, could have a substantial impact on increasing their achievement (Hanushek, Kain, & Rivkin, 2009). This relationship held even when taking into account other variables such as school quality and peers' achievement. Also, like several other studies, the study found that desegregation negligibly impacted on White achievement scores, leading to the conclusion that decreasing Black segregation may improve Black achievement scores without adversely affecting White achievement scores.

Given the previous findings, it is not surprising that comprehensive reviews of the literature report positive effects from integrated settings and negative ones from segregated learning environments (Braddock & Eitle, 2004; Linn & Welner, 2007; Mickelson, 2008; Vigdore & Ludwig, 2008; Welner, 2006). Importantly, however, findings vary greatly. Effects are generally strongest for high school students, students from disadvantaged minority backgrounds, and those from low-income families. Reading and mathematics findings appear robust and definitive (Mickelson & Bottia, 2010); research focusing on outcomes relating to science, however, remains more tentative, largely because there is less of it. One review of research findings, however, came to a different conclusion (Rossell, Armor, & Walberg, 2001). Still, the general finding emerging from existing studies reveals results that tend to generalize to the reading, language, mathematics, and science outcomes of all racial and ethnic groups.

Despite the previously discussed general findings, research does not always point in the same direction. For example, English-proficient immigrant students perform better in mathematics and science when they attend schools with their coethnics (Mickelson & Bottia, 2010). A national study examined the educational achievement of Latinos in segregated settings (Goldsmith, 2003). The results revealed that segregation leads to disadvantages for Latinos and Blacks, but the proportion of Latino students tends to influence test scores positively during the high school years. The proportion of Black students, in contrast, does not affect test scores except for a negative effect for Blacks in science. Integration of Latinos with Whites would reduce some of the inequalities between schools. It would not have negative effects in some areas; in others, it would help the test scores of Whites but would negatively affect Latinos unless it also replicated some of the helpful features of predominantly Latino schools. These nuances are important, and they may well continue to emerge given that the majority of the studies focus on Black and White students and that little research focuses on increasingly large percentages of other minority youth, such as Latinos/as, Asians, American Indians, and immigrant youth.

Post-Secondary Enrollment

Whether students enroll in post-secondary education constitutes another important related area of research. That research reveals what could be deemed contradictory findings. Some indicate that racially homogeneous learning environments positively affect minority students through, for example, their sense of self-efficacy and aspirations (Frost, 2007; Oates, 2004) and self-esteem (Massey, 2006), and some research finds that immigrant children's expectations associate positively with attending schools with large numbers of coethnics (Wells, 2010). On the other hand, research also shows that attending racially segregated schools diminishes the chances of enrolling in college (Teranishi & Parker, 2010). Yet other research also shows that a high school's mean socioeconomic status influences the chances of attending college, with socioeconomically diverse high schools leading to increased chances of attending college, including the finding that attending college directly relates to the proportion of classmates with highly educated parents (Choi, Raley, Muller, & Riegle-Crumb, 2008).

The general finding relating to race is that there are notable variations by race in how a particular racial and ethnic mix of a diverse school influences the likelihood of attending college (Martin, Karabel, & Jaquez, 2005). This variation in post-secondary enrollments likely is due to a number of factors, such as rigorous curricula, academically oriented peers, and teacher quality, which can vary by the school's racial and socioeconomic profile (Darling-Hammond, 2010; Ehrmann & Massey, 2008; Jackson, 2009; Massey & Fischer, 2006; Yun & Moreno, 2006). Still, research generally confirms that students from racially and socioeconomically integrated settings, especially underserved minority youth, are more likely to attend college (Teranishi & Parker, 2010).

Post-Secondary Academic Performance

Researchers have yet to investigate fully the effects of college performance as it relates to having attended schools with varying degrees of student racial compositions. Instead, the focus has been on the effects of diverse college classrooms and experiences on academic performance (Terenzini, Cabrera, Colbeck, Bjorklund, & Parenti, 2001). That research has tended to find that integrated college experiences relate positively to cognitive development as indexed by academic performance (Bowman, 2010). Despite these important findings, the general lack of research in this area renders them tentative. Research has yet to confirm the long-term academic performance effects of attending schools with varying ethnic compositions.

Fostering Civic Engagement

Increasing integration in schools and classrooms relates to the state's interest in fostering civic engagement. This would be done by producing an educational environment that "reflects the 'pluralistic society' in which our children will live" and "create[s] citizens better prepared to know, to understand, and to work with people of all races and backgrounds, thereby furthering the kind of democratic government our Constitution foresees" (*Parents Involved*, 2007, p. 843). The belief is that growing up in diverse environments prepares students to want to engage in those environments.

The link may be intuitively appealing, but little rigorous research examines the effect of diverse schools and classrooms on outcomes relating to democratic values and civic engagement in the sense of how diverse educational experiences socialize students for their roles as members in complex, multiethnic, and democratic societies. Understanding the potential effects requires examining at least two important areas of research. The first involves the direct effects on civic engagement measures such as voting, community service, and public service. The second addresses more attitudinal and normative dimensions, such as understanding the perspective of others, negotiating conflicts, and exchanging divergent views. The general conclusion that emerges is that the existing empirical record is ambiguous with respect to the proposition that integrated K–12 education fosters democratic civic engagement.

Civic-Minded Attitudes

Research has examined the long-term effects of diverse schools on understanding racial differences and the place of race in the lives of others and in broader society. This area of research, mainly stemming from qualitative work, reports similar findings. A study of six integrated US high school graduates in 1980 reported that integration fostered a deeper understanding of other groups and greater comfort in interracial settings and also that they were better prepared for a racially plural society given their having attended integrated schools (Holmes, Wells, & Revilla, 2005; Wells et al., 2009). Students reporting on their pre-college experiences with integrated schooling also report that it predisposed them to attitudes and perspectives that sustain social cohesion in multiethnic societies. For example, one study concluded that students with substantial experience interacting with diverse peers are more likely to view the world from someone else's perspective and value the importance of diversity (Hurtado, 2005; Hurtado, Engberg, Ponjuan, & Landerman, 2002). These findings are of significance, but their obvious limitations (e.g., the selection of participants and the focus on recalling experiences) leave much to be desired.

Research on espousing values and attitudes consistent with democratic society's ideals largely has been conducted with older adolescents, namely college students. Studies of university students find that interactions with diverse college peers change attitudinal, cognitive, and democratic values as well as cultural awareness and concern for the public good. For example, students entering college with substantial prior interactions with diverse peers are more likely to value the importance of engaging in social action to create social change (Hurtado, 2005; Hurtado et al., 2002). While in college, students involved in diversity experiences are more likely to express democratic sentiments, to take the perspective of others, and to see commonality in values across cultures (Gurin et al., 2002). Similarly, structured diversity experiences contribute to more complex thinking about controversial issues in manners that prepare students for more effective debating of issues and negotiating of conflicts (Gurin, Nagda, & Lopez, 2004). Experience with diversity appears to foster civic concerns and abilities to engage in democratic action, and it is important to highlight that it is individuals' own interactions with racial diversity that appear more effective at promoting civic engagement than curricular and co-curricular experiences (for a review, see Bowman, 2011).

The limited number of studies that have focused on high school students report findings similar to those based on college students. Studies using large data sets of major US cities reveal that a diverse school composition promotes democratic values and positive attitudes toward civic engagement. A series of studies investigating civic attitudes in major US cities examined high school students' values and attitudes toward democracy, civic engagement, and awareness of respect for cultural differences (Kurlaender & Yun, 2001, 2005, 2007). The studies found that attending diverse high schools promotes greater comfort with diverse peers and their perspectives, although there are significant racial and ethnic differences in students' comfort levels. Similarly, reviews have concluded that racially, ethnically, and socioeconomically diverse schools lead to educational outcomes that undergird the attitudinal antecedents to and structural conditions for social cohesion in multiethnic, democratic societies (Mickelson & Nkomo, 2012).

Despite the relatively modest amount of research focusing on adolescents, it is important to highlight that perhaps the strongest evidence of the importance of diversity for the formation of civic attitudes during adolescence derives from research that focuses on the effects of diversity experiences during college. That research reveals that the outcomes of diversity experiences found at the college level, such as those noted previously, are greatly influenced by pre-college experiences. This research demonstrates the limits of what post-secondary schools can do. Although they may influence outcomes, the pre-college experiences influence the magnitude of college diversity experiences on such civic factors as social/political activism and political views (Pascarella, Salisbury, Martin, & Blaich, 2012).

Societal outcomes, such as the ability to participate in an increasingly diverse democratic society, rarely have been explored. The failure to explore this aspect of civic development is somewhat surprising given that outcomes associated with enhancing citizenship have long been established as a primary purpose for public education. The higher education literature that does exist relating to these outcomes suggests that students educated in diverse settings are better able to participate in an increasingly racially diverse and complex democratic environment (Gurin et al., 2002). This general proposition is consistent with data revealing that students of all racial and ethnic groups who attend more diverse schools report stronger support for post-secondary participation and an increased sense of civic engagement compared to their more segregated peers. Students who attend multiracial schools, including Whites, report a high level of desire to live and work with people different from themselves. Students report that they feel prepared to interact and participate in democratic processes with people who are different from themselves, and they further report that they believe school experiences have increased their desire and ability to do so (Kurlaender & Yun, 2005). These are the types of findings worthy of further investigation, especially to determine the nuances surrounding them, such as the factors contributing to the student diversity.

Despite the need for more research, current studies already show that schools with multiethnic student bodies can foster less civic-minded behaviors. Diverse student bodies can be, for example, sites of cross-racial tensions and conflict (Eitle & Eitle, 2003). School integration among middle school students increases perceptions of both friendliness and conflict among students of different racial and ethnic groups (Goldsmith, 2004). Integrated schools and classrooms may experience higher levels of racial and ethnic tension and hence less positive interracial relationships compared to environments with relatively small minority populations (see, e.g., research on victimization: Hanish & Guerra, 2000; Vervoot, Scholte, & Overbeek, 2010). On the other hand, schools can structure intergroup contact, such as through the elimination of tracking, enhancing group work, and installing a multicultural curriculum, in ways that can create conditions that reduce tensions and foster cross-race friendships (Lotan, 2004).

Civic and Political Participation

Education may be critical to democratic citizenship, but the links between education and such fundamentals as voting remain obscure. Particularly in the United States, voter turnout is infamously low, especially for youth. How the propensity to vote is influenced by characteristics of schools and classrooms in which students learn has not been the subject of much empirical research, let alone the subject of research investigating the potential effects of integrated schooling on voting.

In some ways, the lack of research is expected given that many youth actually lack full suffrage—they have neither the right to vote nor the right to hold elected office. Given students' reduced political and civic opportunities, researchers have focused on other forms of participation and intensions to participate. One researcher conducted an important series of studies using data from the International Association for the Evaluation of Educational Achievement's Civic Education Study. Those studies found that racial diversity corresponds to a lower level of political discussion in the classroom and that less political discussion, in turn, correlates with a lower likelihood of adolescents' stated intention of becoming an informed voter (Campbell, 2007). Similarly, other research revealed that racial compositions of schools do not relate to the propensity to vote but that students show a greater propensity to vote when they are from schools with higher political homogeneity (Campbell, 2005, 2006, 2009). Together, this line of research reveals that homogeneous schools and classrooms propel greater civic participation.

The previously discussed rather consistent findings gain support from other studies. One considerably large study (of 52 Chicago high schools) examined the effects of civics education on norms of civic participation, including the commitment to participate (Kahne, Chi, & Middaugh, 2006). That study found that the socioeconomic and racial composition of schools did not influence the outcomes of civic education.

The inconsistency between the promise and reality of integrated schooling and findings about its influence on civic participation is now a well-accepted finding. For example, examinations of the reasons explaining the lack of effect attribute it to a disjunction between the ideals of democracy that is learned (as fair, neutral governments dedicated to equality and freedom) and the reality faced by diverse youth (racial and ethnic injustices) (Junn, 2004). Some identify the promises of democracy as being distant from the lives of immigrants, minorities, and the poor, which renders individuals from disadvantaged communities suspicious of and less likely to engage in civic behaviors such as voting; they view it as the paradox of integration (Oliver, 2010). Researchers may not understand well the reasons for these effects, but research clearly reveals that diversity in schooling does not necessarily lead to civic participation.

Increasing Occupational Attainment

Among the compelling interests used to support diversity initiatives in higher education is the interest in preparing youth for diverse workplaces needed to compete in a global marketplace as well as within the United States. The argument is that diverse workplaces demand cross-cultural experience and understanding gained from diverse educations. These interests may be strong, but it remains unclear whether or how they transfer to the primary and secondary school contexts. The government's interest in fostering diversity experiences to enhance participation in the workplace may be less critical at lower levels of education. Still, research from integrated high schools reveals similar results found in higher education. However, the results can vary considerably, which reduces confidence in identifying settled conclusions.

National studies illustrate the wide variety of findings in this area. One nationally representative study found that high school composition was a significant predictor of co-worker racial mix (Braddock & McPartland, 1989). Another nationally representative study reported that exposure to diverse racial groups in high school reduced racial isolation in the post-high school workplace (Stearns, 2010). Importantly, the study reported considerable variation. The high school racial mix did not have a significant influence on the workplace racial isolation of Asian American and Latinos; for them, the racial isolation in their neighborhoods had a significant influence. For White students, exposure to Asian Americans, African Americans, and Latinos had the effect of reducing racial isolation in their workplace, whereas for African Americans, it was exposure to Latinos and Whites. Another study found that Blacks who attended high schools with higher proportions of White students had fewer Black co-workers, whereas White students who attended high schools with higher proportions of White students tended to have higher proportions of White co-workers (Stearns, 2010). No simple rules emerge from these studies examining the effects of diverse schools on working in diverse occupational environments, with perhaps the best conclusion being that links are far from direct and depend on numerous other factors.

Understanding the Pervasive Lack of Expected Effects

Given the harms popularly attributed to segregation, it likely was reasonable to expect desegregation to result in ameliorating effects. However, the available research revealed mixed effects. Integration efforts also have produced mixed effects. The failure to reach conclusive and supportive findings is troubling because of researchers' claims; the massive amount of research in this area; and the expectation that, by now, the empirical evidence should be clear. However, many reasons can explain the lack of expected support.

Anti-Classification Findings

The anti-classification approach embraces desegregation efforts as the most justifiable rationale for addressing harms of segregation. However, the available evidence fails to support that remedy. The self-esteem of Blacks rarely increases in desegregated schools, and it actually appears already high in the first place. The achievement level of Blacks sometimes increases and rarely decreases in desegregated schools; but their achievement aspirations when they are in segregated schools actually appear to be higher than those of Whites in segregated schools. Desegregation generally does not reduce prejudices, particularly of Whites toward Blacks, and it leads to increases in Black prejudice toward Whites approximately as frequently as it leads to decreases. These findings are not as powerful and affirming as reform efforts might have expected, and they certainly do not seem strong enough to marshal the dramatic educational changes sought by *Brown*. Although this is not to say that desegregation should not occur, a fair examination of existing studies does reveal that empirical research fails to support the legal system's rationales.

The research findings relating to desegregation may be disappointing, but it is important to consider why the research has identified so few strong and expected effects. The research can be viewed best as tentative. Most of the studies investigated only the short-term effects of desegregation, such as data gathered during one year and typically quite early in the implementation of desegregation plans. The extent and type of desegregation varied greatly. The studies were conducted in different regions of the United States and with children of different ages and different educational experiences. The studies also often used incomparable measures, which makes difficult any systematic analyses. In addition, studies typically did not include what would now be common control variables, such as social class and IQ. As many reviews have noted, older syntheses suffered from flawed research designs or reported results from incompletely implemented desegregation plans (Bradley & Bradley, 1977; Gerard & Miller, 1975; Linn & Welner, 2007; Mickelson, 2008). Given the limitations of existing research, it is not surprising that the results often varied considerably or actually were not supportive of desegregation.

Research findings may be limited, but even if they were more robust, it is not clear what the findings would mean. The findings likely remain contentious given that the reasons for the findings themselves remain unclear. Studies relating to academic achievement, what appear to be the most robust findings reporting positive outcomes of desegregation, remain contentious for the simple reason that academic gains, chiefly defined by test scores, do not reveal the underlying reasons for these gains (or lack of them). Multiple factors may account for academic achievement.

Academic achievement may be due to schools' resources and students' friendships. Students' improved achievement in integrated schools appears related to the resources to help improve learning opportunities that are more likely to be found in schools with greater proportions of non-minority students. In addition, students' motivation to succeed academically significantly relates to their social relationships with others, social skills, and social competence (Wentzel, 1989; Wigfield & Eccles, 2002). Achievement levels of close friends significantly relate to adolescents' own academic outcomes for all races and ethnicities (Ryan, 2000; Shin, Daly, & Vera, 2007). However, the importance of access to same-ethnic peers can vary. For example, African American and Asian youth benefit more from the mere presence of a heterogeneous mix and access to same-race/ethnic group peers compared to White or Hispanic adolescents; White and Hispanic youth appear to benefit more from friendships than from general access to same-race/ethnic groups (Ueno, 2009). Both of these findings are significant given that schools may be segregated internally. The nature of the school, particularly how it shapes relationships, influences outcomes.

Factors not directly relating to school resources and dynamics also may influence outcomes and challenge the assumption that integrated schools produce positive outcomes. Much has been written about the potential negative consequences of high academic achievement among Black youth (e.g., "acting White"; Fordham & Ogbu, 1986; Fryer & Torelli, 2006). The basis for this assumption is that Black youth who are high achievers in school face negative peer consequences, including being accused of trying to be better than others or "acting White." The extent to which this process actually occurs in schools remains contentious (Buck, 2010), and the negative consequences of achievement for students of color may arise only in integrated schools (Fryer & Torelli, 2006). Nonetheless, this area of research highlights potential negative consequences for youth of color when they act in ways that seem inconsistent among family or peers. Thus, as the most robust example of desegregation's positive effects illustrates, the reason for the effects may be due to other factors, and other factors operating in schools may work to counter potentially positive effects.

The inconsistent findings also are not surprising given the nature of desegregation. Desegregation developed in a variety of ways, which influenced its effectiveness. Desegregation resisted by community leaders and schools likely did not produce the intended positive effects. Even when not resisted, desegregation likely was not undertaken in ways to maximize its effectiveness. Indeed, researchers who have reviewed the research on desegregation's effects have argued that social scientists in the 1960s and 1970s misdirected their efforts by focusing on the confusing outcomes of desegregation because desegregation occurred under conditions that would minimize its effectiveness. In a real sense, comprehensive research that would help explain how desegregation could result in the most positive outcomes emerged only after research indicated that desegregation pervasively did not lead to the intended positive effects. This new emphasis focused more on situational factors, such as the contextual and process factors that characterize particular desegregated settings. That research would follow the elements identified by a leading expert on prejudice, Allport (1954), and would focus on such elements as equal-status contact, norms favorable to intergroup relationships, close cross-race exposure, the presence of individuals who counteract racial stereotypes, and task interdependence. Research examining the effects of these factors, however, generally derives from schools that were not desegregated by legal mandate (Longshore & Prager, 1985).

Arguably the strongest reason for the lack of expected outcomes relates to the inability of desegregation alone to effect dramatic changes. Schools may be important sources of influence on youth, but multiple socializing institutions, both formal and informal, influence youth development. As a result, altering one critical factor in children's schooling may not enhance their self-esteem, improve intergroup relationships, or raise their academic achievement. These outcomes are highly influenced by families, communities, and general societal forces such as economic conditions and opportunities.

The lack of consistent and positive effects likely will continue. Many districts have abandoned desegregation plans. Since the 1990s, schools increasingly have been declared "unitary," rendering them free from court oversight because they no longer are segregated by district policy. Once declared unitary, districts must dismantle their desegregation programs (Orfield & Lee, 2004). This development likely means an end to research in this area given the decrease in the districts under court orders to desegregate.

Anti-subordination Findings

Anti-subordination research—research that moves beyond examining the effects of formal segregation and desegregation—differs dramatically from anti-classification research by at least one factor. Despite considerable diversity in findings and areas of inquiry, the findings are much more supportive of diversity and integration. Diversity of viewpoints and academic success are clear examples of benefits, but much depends on the nature of the implementation, such as the school climate, socioeconomic statuses, and the involved ethnic/racial groups. The major reasons put forth for differences in findings have to do with the nature of the studies. Older syntheses suffer from flawed research designs or from incompletely implemented desegregation plans (Bradley & Bradley, 1977; Gerard & Miller, 1975; Linn & Welner, 2007; Mickelson, 2008). It is true that later studies use impressive data, but the studies still have both strengths and weaknesses, with the weaknesses often overshadowing the strengths.

The strengths of recent studies, those that address subjugation more broadly, are rather impressive. Recent studies make greater use of control variables to understand the sources of effects. Likewise, recent studies focus on the effects of desegregation plans or school diversity long after they have been implemented, and they also use different statistical tools that permit more accurate analyses. Many of these studies make use of high-quality survey data sets that benefit from large, representative samples. These data sets use sophisticated measures of achievement outcomes and have high-quality indicators of individual student characteristics (including prior achievement), family background (e.g., parents' education and occupations), school quality (e.g., teacher characteristics), and classroom factors (e.g., peer effects) known to affect outcomes. Large data sets also increasingly permit longitudinal analyses over time, which permit researchers to use sophisticated statistical techniques to test causal models that distinguish among student, family, school, and neighborhood factors that shape effects. The richer data increase the likelihood that the findings from these studies will be more useful and more fine-tuned. The now classic example of these advances is the ability to use multilevel modeling to tease out different units of analysis (e.g., schools, individuals, classrooms, neighborhoods, districts, and states) nested in one another, which permits controlling for factors that lead to biased estimates.

Despite new studies' strengths, however, they may have attenuated legal relevance. For example, research uses the terms *desegregated* and *integrated* interchangeably. When understood in light of the focus that the legal system places on segregation by law or de facto segregation, research fails to inform legal disputes because it does not allow for disentangling the effects of governmental actions. In fact, some studies do not even address those issues; they instead focus on racial balancing in schools. Without clearly articulating these nuances, then, at the outset, important difficulties emerge in efforts to address legal issues. The significance of governmental action is that regardless of the robustness of research demonstrating that the races are situated differentially, research findings simply run the risk of irrelevance in the absence of direct state action causing the differential treatment effects under study. Thus, and following this line of legal reasoning, regardless of the amount of research conducted in this area, much of it potentially remains irrelevant.

In addition to issues of relevance, even research using the best available techniques and large data sets does not necessarily support expected outcomes. The failure to find benefits of integration on civic development is illustrative. The lack of findings may be due to the extent to which many important non-academic outcomes fall outside the logic of conventional measurement, such as the consequences of civic education for a democracy (Ladwig, 2010; McNeil, 1986). In addition to substantive knowledge and skills, civic education's outcomes include dispositions that are difficult to conceptualize and index. The challenge of knowing exactly what to measure is exacerbated when seeking to understand the factors that would influence it—not knowing what to measure is a problem for examining the effects of such factors as integrated schooling.

Despite challenges, some key factors have been identified; but even they are difficult to consider fully. For example, school climate, such as how schools recognize rights and foster equality, has an impact on such factors as violence in schools and academic outcomes. It would be difficult to downplay the potential role of school climate, even though it is difficult to pinpoint its effects. Other important factors include inequalities in the political and economic structure of society and the structural constraints that discourage participation in democracies, such as through voting and commitment to political equality and embracing democratic norms (Gutmann, 1999). These factors matter. However, even increasingly well-researched areas of study may not be able to discern the complexity of phenomena, let alone their relationships to specific factors such as racial diversity.

Conclusions

A close examination of empirical research relating to differential treatment based on group status reveals striking findings. They are striking because they challenge long-held beliefs of how society should educate youth from different ethnic/racial backgrounds. This is not to say that current policy choices are misguided or simply wrong. However, it is to say that the legal rationales supporting policy approaches do not appear to gain much support from existing research.

Existing empirical evidence generally fails to support the narrow, anti-classification arguments raised in *Brown* regarding the effects of segregation and the rationales that support the desegregation of schools. In fact, research rejecting segregation on the rationales articulated in *Brown*, such as self-esteem effects, actually is quite weak. In addition, some of the more robust research findings actually do not support *Brown's* rationales for engaging in desegregation efforts. Some of the positive effects of desegregation may not result from the law's racial attributions but, rather, from other factors. The positive effects of desegregation on academic achievement relate to the socioeconomic status of students and schools, and race relations have much to do with a particular school's social climate. Depending on a variety of factors, both segregation and desegregation can lead to unexpected outcomes. This makes for a point worth repeating: The now dominant legal approach to addressing diversity in schools rests on permitting the use of racial classifications to diversify schools only when the government desegregated. Research has difficulty supporting the legally recognized harms of segregation and the benefits of desegregation.

Research that lends itself to examining whether more anti-subordination approaches would reach effectiveness also reveals equivocal findings. Support largely varies because much depends on the nature of the legally recognized compelling interests that support the need for considering race/ethnicity when assigning children to particular schools. In some contexts, for example, racially balanced schools foster the structural and attitudinal antecedents for the development of a socially cohesive, just, multiethnic, democratic society; they also can foster academic achievement. Much research supports the claim that communities have important interests in furthering more informed responses to diversity and in engaging in policymaking that considers the subordination of groups. Regrettably, the legal system does not fully embrace those interests; they may not be compelling enough to support race-conscious policies.

The conclusions presented here are challenging. Research does not send a clear message to support widely held beliefs about equality. Nor does research unequivocally support specific policies. The diversity in findings mirrors the different views held by members of the Supreme Court. As expected from research investigating complex human phenomena, much depends on contexts and nuances not lending themselves to broad pronouncements.

5

Empirical Assessments of the Implementation of Laws Addressing School Segregation and Diversity

The Significance of the Implementation of Laws

The hazards inherent in the government's treating individuals differently based on their race require much more than demonstrating compelling reasons for treating groups differently. The government also must show the necessity for differential treatment to achieve its goals. This means that before grouping people into different racial classifications, the government must demonstrate that it considered race-neutral alternatives and found those alternatives insufficient. In addition, if group-based distinctions are needed to further compelling goals, the government must reach them in ways that least infringe on people's rights. Infringement on the right to equal treatment must be as minimal as possible because the government's treating groups of people differently is a suspect way to enhance equality or achieve other governmental goals. By assuring that the government's goals warrant the use of the highly suspect tool of using race-conscious policies, the Court seeks to "smoke out" illegitimate uses of race. The upshot is that the implementation of laws and policies matters as much as the reasons for treating people differently to ensure equality.

The twin requirements for the proper implementation of race-conscious laws and policies—consideration of alternatives and minimal rights infringements—raise empirical issues and actually require empirical analyses. The Court's evaluations require the government to demonstrate the legitimacy of its actions. Regrettably, the Court has left unclear what constitutes appropriate consideration of alternatives and minimal infringements. Still, the Court has developed analyses that allow for determining whether and how empirical evidence might address them. An examination of those ways can lead to important conclusions. Available evidence can demonstrate the legal system's challenges when it requires empirical findings for formulating policies and making administrative decisions. It also can shed light on the potential effectiveness of race-neutral alternatives and the nature of minimal intrusions.

Addressing Race-Neutral Alternatives

The government's use of racial categories may be inherently suspect and call for considering alternative measures, but what that consideration entails remains vague and challenging to address. Different justices hold different views. This diversity means that empirical analyses may become relevant in a variety of ways, or they may end up ignored. As a result, it also means that analyses of the potential influence of empirical findings must first work through potential legal approaches and then consider the extent to which they invite empirical analyses that would be both doable and useful.

What the Law Requires

The leading case involving primary and secondary education, *Parents Involved in Community Schools v. Seattle School District No. 1* (2007), fails to provide an appropriate starting point regarding the implementation of laws or policies that would treat people differently by race. In that case, the Court rejected the government's rationales for treating people differently. Instead, it found the schools' plans directed only to racial balance, pure and simple—an objective that the Court again condemned as illegitimate. The Court refused to consider possible rationales supporting the need for racial diversity, as the school districts apparently had not considered them when enacting their policies. As a result, the Court stopped short of requiring the government to have considered alternatives to using racial classifications before adopting the school assignment programs. Chief Justice Roberts' plurality opinion sidestepped further analyses by asserting that the school districts' plans were not narrowly tailored. He stated that the debate about the benefits of diversity "is not one we need to resolve, however, because it is clear that the racial classifications employed by the districts are not narrowly tailored" (*Parents Involved*, 2007, p. 726). *Parents Involved* reinforces the lesson that accepting the government's reasons for treating people according to their racial status leads to the need to consider how the government implements that treatment. Understanding how the Court will address implementation issues requires a turn to a line of closely related cases dealing with post-secondary education.

In the schooling context, *Grutter v. Bollinger* (2003) clearly explained the Court's approach to requiring the government to have considered alternatives to using racial classifications. In her opinion for the Court, Justice

O'Connor outlined the steps that the government, in this case state universities, must take prior to using race/ethnicity in their admission decisions. She noted that

> narrow tailoring does not require exhaustion of every conceivable race-neutral alternative. Nor does it require a university to choose between maintaining a reputation for excellence or fulfilling a commitment to provide educational opportunities to members of all racial groups. . . . Narrow tailoring does, however, require serious, good faith consideration of workable race-neutral alternatives that will achieve the diversity the university seeks. (p. 339)

In addition, she noted that "race conscious admissions policies must be limited in time," which she expected to be 25 years until the use of racial preferences no longer would be necessary (p. 342). Although the 25 years was conjecture that would not even be tested, it was a necessary part of the ruling. Not having a logical end would mean that the government would continue racial distinctions. Continuing distinctions was problematic because doing so effectively would thwart the ultimate goal of eliminating racial considerations in governmental decision-making. Although allowing for race-conscious policies, then, the Court emphasized that they should be temporary fixed used sparingly.

Ten years after *Grutter*, the Court re-examined the matter in *Fisher I* (*Fisher v. the University of Texas*, 2013). In that case, the Supreme Court determined that the lower court had not held the university to the demanding burden of strict scrutiny articulated in earlier cases. In remanding the case, at least seven justices agreed that

> the Fifth Circuit must assess whether the University has offered sufficient evidence to prove that its admissions program is narrowly tailored to obtain the educational benefits of diversity. . . . University must prove [to the reviewing court] that the means it chose to attain that diversity are narrowly tailored to its goal. On this point, the University receives no deference. . . . *The reviewing court must ultimately be satisfied that no workable race-neutral alternatives would produce the educational benefits of diversity.* (p. 2414, emphasis added)

The *Fisher I* decision yielded a greater degree of legal stability. It declares that the government receives no deference and that the government must demonstrate that no workable alternative exists to achieving the goals for adopting race-conscious policies. In doing so, the Court heavily burdens the government's efforts to develop policies that take into account individuals' race.

The high burden placed on the government likely explains why the Court left the door open to race-conscious mechanisms when so many commentators had expected more conservative justices to overturn the *Grutter* decision and strike down affirmative action in post-secondary school admissions. The Court significantly narrowed situations allowing for the legitimate use of race-conscious policies. When the Court revisited *Fisher* in 2016 (*Fisher II: Fisher v. the University of Texas*, 2016), it examined the university's efforts to increase diversity and concluded that no alternative approaches considered or discussed during the course of litigation indicated workable means through which the university could reach its educational goals. Importantly, even though the Court upheld the university's policy, it emphasized that the university had undertaken the obligation to use data to scrutinize and refine its admissions policies and that it had presented extensive evidence of race-neutral efforts that had failed to obtain the benefits the university sought. However, vagueness still remains, particularly in terms of alternative approaches because the best guidance we have is from post-secondary education and that guidance remains vague. The vagueness is important to understand because it complicates efforts to create and use empirical analyses to inform legal positions.

Workable Alternative Approaches

The Court has not clearly stated what constitutes "workable." Workable suggests that race-neutral alternatives would not have too great of an adverse effect on other governmental objectives, such as maintaining the "quality" of a student body or educational experiences. If challenged, the government must convince a court that race-neutral alternatives are unworkable because the costs of such policies would be too great. However, the reviewing court apparently retains the discretion to determine how great those costs would be. In addition, *Fisher II* appears to have recast *Grutter's* requirement of good faith consideration of race-neutral alternatives into a more stringent exhaustion requirement. Under *Fisher II*, no workable alternative can exist. The first time the Court addressed the issue in *Fisher I* (2013, p. 2420), Justice Kennedy had tempered the exhaustion of alternatives requirement with the caveat that a nonracial approach must produce the educational benefits of diversity "about as well and at tolerable administrative expense." When the Court revisited *Fisher I* (*Fisher II*, 2016), Justice Kennedy would briefly review proposed alternatives and find that the university had exhausted other approaches in its efforts to meet educational goals. The effort to temper requirements makes for a vague standard: "tolerable" or "works as well" or even "exhaust other alternatives" can leave much to different interpretations.

The lack of clarity in standards creates obstacles to effectively using empirical findings; it even fails to provide guidance as to the usefulness of research. It may well be that the required analysis calls for simple accounting rather than, for example, complex research designs and variables detailing benefits such as reduced hostility among groups and increased academic achievement specifically attributable to the alternatives used. However, at its core, the last-resort inquiry would entail a thorough examination of possible race-neutral alternatives, require empirical evidence to indicate that race is not a dominant factor in the chosen policy, and look unfavorably on race-conscious policies that have small effects on reaching its goals by using racial classifications (few youth would be affected by the policy). Not all justices would agree with the need to even consider last-resort inquiries. However, if they were needed, their components appear rather straightforward.

Discerning the legal system's core needs may be helpful, but even it still leaves much undetermined. It remains to be determined what facts must be presented to satisfy a court that the government found no workable race-neutral alternatives. Also left open is the degree of certainty needed to satisfy the reviewing court. In addition, the threshold for tolerable expense or the line between tolerable and intolerable expense is also unknown. Also left undetermined are the nature of costs that matter—schools have complex missions that consider factors ranging from individual academic, social, health, and civic to economic development as well as to broader public health and fiscal matters coupled by a variety of parental concerns such as child safety, location, peer influences, school extracurricular activities, and the school's reputation. The flexibility may be needed, but this area of study reveals that reasonable people can hold vastly different opinions when dealing with these matters.

Race-Neutral Approaches

The Supreme Court's decisions are likewise vague regarding what "race-neutral" denotes. Vagueness remains even though the Court endorses the use of neutral alternatives and actually requires their consideration. The *Grutter* (2003) decision obliquely makes the following reference:

> Universities in California, Florida, and Washington State, where racial preferences in admissions are prohibited by state law, are currently engaged in experimenting with a wide variety of alternative approaches. Universities in other States can and should draw on the most promising aspects of these race-neutral alternatives as they develop. (p. 342)

In recognizing the possibility that some alternatives could be developed, the Court avoids ruling on the legitimacy of particular alternatives while it simultaneously mandates their consideration.

Although understood as possible, race-neutral alternatives raise tricky issues. Neutral alternatives are of significance beyond the possibility that they could point to effective means that do not use protected classifications. They also attract a different level of evaluation. Unlike neutral categories, these alternatives do not trigger strict scrutiny. By not triggering a high standard of review, these approaches to addressing inequality are more likely to be found legally permissible. Although the notion of neutral governmental activities may be disputable, actions deemed neutral gain considerable legitimacy and support.

Again, however, the Court opened the door but remains vague in practice. The Court has not held that race-neutral policies intended to benefit groups that constitute protected classifications are exempt from strict scrutiny. The Court remains concerned about hidden racial motivations because they may be even more worrisome than explicit racially motivated legislation given that they are less amenable to public, administrative, and judicial scrutiny. Also, the Court has rejected precisely this form of subterfuge, as it has explained that "statutes are subject to strict scrutiny . . . not just when they contain express racial classifications, but also when, though race-neutral on their face, they are motivated by a racial purpose or object" (*Miller v. Johnson*, 1995, p. 913). For this reason, facially race-neutral programs motivated by a racially discriminatory purpose and resulting in a racially discriminatory effect may be subject to strict scrutiny if they are instituted primarily to achieve racially conscious goals. Policies typically are deemed "race-conscious" if they would not have been promulgated but for the motivation for achieving segregation or racial impact, race is the predominant motivating factor behind the policy, or the race-neutral criteria are deliberately used as a proxy for race. It would seem that any policy that gives weight in admissions decisions to any other factors aside from race (e.g., socioeconomic status) with the goal of boosting diversity would not be deemed "race-neutral"; it would be deemed "race-conscious" and face the strict scrutiny test.

The Court's evasiveness may be peculiar, but it also appears necessary. An inherent tension exists between the need to be "race-neutral" and the need to take an "alternative" approach. An "alternative" policy to making race-based classifications that serves the same goal may not be deemed "race-neutral." For example, *Fisher I* reveals that after the *Hopwood* decision (*Hopwood v. Texas*, 1996) that challenged the University of Texas School of Law's affirmative action policy, the Texas Legislature enacted H.B. 588. That law gave state institutions a list of 18 socioeconomic indicators that they could use in making first-time freshman admissions decisions. To the extent that the use of such indicators was intended to serve the purpose of replacing race-based affirmative action, such use would not be "race-neutral."

The *Fisher* cases recognized that tension, but each case addressed it differently. In *Fisher I* (2013), the tension was recognized in Justice Ginsburg's lone dissent: "I have said before and reiterate here that only an ostrich could regard the supposedly neutral alternatives as race unconscious. . . . As Justice Souter observed, the vaunted alternatives suffer from 'the disadvantage of deliberate obfuscation'" (pp. 2433–2434). She insisted that "i[t] is race consciousness, not blindness to race, that drives such plans" (*Id.*). However, in the follow-up case (*Fisher II*, 2016), the majority opinion quoted, with approval, Justice Ginsberg's dissent. The Court embraced the Top Ten Percent Plan as a race-conscious plan and used that understanding to reject the argument that relying only on that plan would make the university's admissions more race-neutral. Ultimately, the point is that motivations matter, but it is not clear when they will matter because the majority of the justices are willing to ignore them or fully embrace them. Regardless, justices need to accept that neutral alternatives are theoretically possible and should be considered if for no other reason that finding otherwise simply gives the government the power to engage in race-conscious efforts to address compelling rationales for diversity.

At primary and secondary school levels, *Parents Involved* actually is instructive, even though it too leaves much to be desired. The case offered explicit race-neutral means of achieving governmental goals. In his concurring opinion, Justice Kennedy noted many potentially legitimate ways to increase diversity. He suggested strategically placing schools at particular sites, drawing attendance zones on the basis of neighborhood demographics, funding special programs, targeting the recruitment of faculty and students, and using statistical procedures to track education (*Parents Involved*, 2007, p. 789). In his view, these approaches would offer a richer and more flexible decision-making approach not based on race alone. They also would have the benefit of not focusing on individual youth. Although endorsing these mechanisms, Kennedy did not contend that race-neutral actions exist free from potentially serious harms. Instead, he stated that these "measures that do not rely on differential treatment based on individual classifications present these problems to a lesser degree" (*Id*., pp. 796–797).

Despite being offered helpful suggestions for achieving the benefits of diversity without directly making individual racial classifications, the dissenting justices found such alternative means unviable. For example, Justice Breyer was unable to identify "reasonably evident alternatives" by which the districts could reach their goals for diversity (*Id*., p. 850). As a result, more than the other justices, he was willing to defer to the local school boards'

> knowledge, expertise, and concerns in these particular matters . . . since judges are not well suited to act as school administrators . . . [and] local school boards better understand their own communities and have a better knowledge of what in practice will best meet the educational needs of their pupils. (*Id*., p. 849)

The lack of alternatives makes race-conscious mechanisms feasible. It does so even despite conflicting research supporting rationales for race-conscious policies. Local decision makers are deemed best suited to sort through evidence to do what is best for their communities.

Justice Breyer's approach reveals how a court that would embrace race-conscious efforts could address empirical findings. His analysis points to diversity as a goal as well as the benefits that would come from it. In doing so, he was the justice who reviewed the most empirical research and fully embraced it. His review found conflicting evidence regarding diversity's benefits relating to academic gains; and he also found disagreement about diversity's effects on furthering democratic interests in reducing prejudice and increasing cooperation among all races. Rather than reject efforts due to conflicting evidence, he would leave them to the discretion of local decision makers on the rationale that the conflicting evidence means that their decisions could be deemed reasonable. It is this type of analysis that other justices reject; they seek more certainty that the government needs race-conscious policies and can implement them appropriately. Justice Breyer appears less bothered by such considerations as long as the policies are for benign reasons, a view flatly rejected by justices who dismiss the ability to discern the benign nature of race-conscious policies.

As expected, different positions about workable alternatives have real consequences—both for policies and for the role of empirical evidence. Not having alternatives tips the balance in favor of using protected classifications rather than acting neutrally toward them. The alternate position is also true: Identifying neutral alternatives reduces the chances of supporting the use of protected classifications. Regardless of the positions taken, then, the legal system invites empirical analyses. Despite that invitation, the legal system allows for different interpretations of those findings and even different interpreters. Under one approach, the Court would give close scrutiny to the empirical findings; under another approach, the Court would give the government (local decision makers) discretion to use the findings to act reasonably. As the lively analyses in *Parents Involved* reveal, these approaches can result in widely different outcomes.

Empirical Findings and Challenges

Empirically, several areas of research relating to potentially neutral alternatives have received attention. All of these mechanisms have been instituted to achieve diversity, sometimes even by using racial classifications to determine school assignments. Although the measures sometimes have been couched as efforts to counter segregation, sometimes they are presented in terms of the need to reach the benefits of diversity rather than create diversity itself. Whether these motivations will matter remains to be seen, but such motivations likely will not matter if the government cannot document the mechanisms' effectiveness in achieving diversity or its related benefits.

Socioeconomic Status as a Proxy for Race

Rather than use race to determine school assignments, socioeconomic status may serve as the criterion to develop assignment plans that support diversity and its hoped-for outcomes. These approaches have garnered much interest, particularly because they could be problematic. Although they often are presented as viable and intuitively appealing alternatives, existing research reveals their limitations. Generally, proposed economic-based alternatives are limited for two related reasons.

First, income distributions do not serve as good proxies because they overlap substantially with racial status. The overlap would seem to support the effectiveness of using income as a proxy. However, it does not: The potentially close relationship between race and income generally fails to serve as a strong proxy. Socioeconomic proxy programs would work best in circumstances with wide disparities in income based on race, and this has been found to be the case. Districts in locations without wide disparities do not produce strong racial effects when school assignments rely on socioeconomic status (Reardon, Yun, & Kurlaender, 2006). The point is that districts tend to lack sufficient variation based on socioeconomic status to create a difference similar to what would be achieved by using race itself.

Second, districts would need racial diversity as they would socioeconomic diversity. That is, locations need enough racial diversity to make a difference in the first instance. Relying on socioeconomic status remains considerably limited in contexts without a large enough population and space that would accommodate assignments needed for racial balancing. Racial income inequality and income segregation in urban districts likely further high levels of racial segregation under any practical income-integration policy. Given the extent of residential racial segregation, race-neutral income-integration policies likely will not significantly reduce school racial segregation.

Even if socioeconomic status could be used as a proxy for race, its use may not foster intended outcomes. Longitudinal studies indicate that mixing socioeconomic groups in schools does not necessarily lead to lifting everyone's educational achievement and may actually have negative effects. Nationally representative, longitudinal studies reveal that as the proportion of the student body with middle- or high-income parents increases, low-income students progress less far in math and science (Crosnoe, 2009). These findings concur with the widely observed second-generation segregation that occurs within schools due to tracking, disability programs, and school discipline (Levesque, 2015). Equally important, as the proportion of the student body with middle- or high-income or college-educated parents increases, low-income students experience more psychosocial problems. These patterns are more pronounced among African American and Latino students. In fact, Whites were the only group of low-income students to demonstrate any benefits of being in schools with more students from higher socioeconomic backgrounds (Crosnoe, 2009). Findings indicating heightened risks for minority students call for caution. Markers of disadvantage, whether they be race or socioeconomic status, deemed as useful for remedying disadvantage continue to play important roles in interventions and run the risk of creating even more disadvantages.

Multiple Individual Indicators as Proxies

Given the limitations of using only socioeconomic status to achieve diversity or its benefits, efforts have been made to complement it with other factors.

These efforts also have been found to be less than effective. In fact, they may end up being counterproductive and even harmful.

Illustrative of the unintended effects of using more individualized factors is the use of academic achievement to determine school assignments. Adding academic achievement to other individual factors results in even less racial diversity (Reardon et al., 2006). Adding factors such as academic ability and achievement is problematic to the extent that they remain intricately related to race and socioeconomic status. For example, substantial differences exist by race and ethnicity in children's test scores as they begin kindergarten. Researchers attribute these differences to factors related to socioeconomic status, such as family structure, educational expectations, and neighborhood conditions—all of which relate to race and ethnicity (Duncan & Magnuson, 2005; Lee & Burkham, 2002). The school readiness gap in racial and ethnic groups relates as strongly to socioeconomic status as it does to the achievement gap that continues and widens throughout educational trajectories. Sorting school assignments by using socioeconomic status and other factors need not improve disadvantaged youth's outcomes.

Magnet Schools

Magnet schools provide specialized curricula in a particular subject area and seek to attract students of different races and socioeconomic backgrounds from local public and private schools. These schools generally are located in high-poverty, racially segregated neighborhoods. They rely on parental choice and different thematic programs to attract wealthier White students from surrounding areas. The desire to create diverse school environments likely is a factor, but programs tend not to explicitly use racial diversity to justify the schools. However, financial support for these programs has come from federal funding initiatives designed to provide an additional or alternative tool (e.g., to redrawn attendance zones and cross-town busing) for districts engaged in court-ordered or voluntary school desegregation efforts (Smrekar & Honey, 2015).

Researchers debate the ability of magnet schools to serve as effective integration tools. In 2003, the US Department of Education conceded that the 57 schools that received magnet school grants for the 1998–2001 cycle "overall . . . made only modest progress in reducing minority group isolation" (Christenson et al., 2003, p. x). Only 57 percent of the grantees succeeded in preventing, eliminating, or reducing minority group isolation, and 35 percent of the schools only reduced minority group isolation by 5 percentage points or less. These figures leave approximately 8 percent of schools—approximately 5 schools out of nearly 60—making a difference above what could be deemed negligible. Whether such percentages suffice to support these programs—given their costs and repercussions on school districts' resources—becomes difficult to discern.

Given the limited ability of most magnet schools to reach diversity goals, researchers have identified conditions that increase the likelihood of success at promoting diversity and avoiding racial isolation. To succeed, magnet schools must use an equitable approach for selecting students and must ensure that families have pertinent and centralized information about the magnet schools offered in the district. Magnet schools also need to provide effective transportation for students. Magnet schools in non-Hispanic, White neighborhoods are more likely to achieve integration than those in minority neighborhoods. Magnet schools with racially and ethnically mixed groups of minority students, involved parents, and a low student–teacher ratio are more likely to reduce racial isolation. Finally, elementary schools and whole-school, rather than within-school, programs more effectively prevent, eliminate, or reduce racial isolation. Although research may reveal what could be effective, it also reveals that magnet schools need considerable support, and several factors must coalesce before schools can produce diversity and its benefits.

Available evidence reveals that the factors needed for effectiveness do not transfer well into practice. One of the most widely cited studies of its kind examined 450 parent transfer requests for admission into elementary magnet school programs in Montgomery County, Maryland, in 1985 (Henig, 1990, 1996). At the time, the school district was operating a voluntary "managed choice" program designed to entice parents to transfer their children from neighborhood schools to thematically focused magnet schools in the predominantly minority section of the county. Transfers were approved (at a rate of 85 percent) unless the move would exacerbate racial isolation or overcrowding; transportation was provided to the magnet school. The study found that transfer requests demonstrated a clear and consistent pattern across both White and minority families in the opposite direction of magnet school policy aims. White families were most likely to select magnet schools that were majority White and located in higher-income neighborhoods. Minority families were also likely to seek cultural familiarity and racial consistency; they tended to select schools that were majority minority and located in lower-income neighborhoods (Henig, 1990, 1996). Even when the choices are controlled and include factors relating to race, they may be ineffective in addressing racial imbalances when individuals can make private choices.

The pattern identified by the Maryland study decades ago continues. In the early 2000s, reviews revealed that magnet school contexts lacked effectiveness in redressing racial imbalances because "race is a primary consideration in school choices" (Saporito, 2003, p. 198). That is, magnet schools would not decrease racial imbalances because, given the choice, parents would prefer racial imbalances for their children's schools. More than a decade later, the most recent review concluded that although parents state that their primary considerations in choosing magnet schools is the academic quality of the school and safety, parents are most attracted to schools with distinctive programs situated in familiar (to the parents) neighborhoods (Smrekar & Honey, 2015). Whether the location of the school is in a predominantly White or predominantly Black neighborhood, research suggests that cultural familiarity and racial consistency matter in the choices that parents make for their children's school assignments (Smrekar & Honey, 2015). Such private choices are permissible, and they may be legally required for these programs, but they do not support the articulated need for magnet schools: the reduction of racial imbalances. Available evidence, then, tends to question the real "workability" and effectiveness of programs that do not explicitly use race in school assignments.

Vouchers and School Choice

Policies giving parents increased choice to determine where to send their children to school, and supporting those choices through vouchers, have increased in popularity. Their popularity has not been matched by their effectiveness in addressing racial imbalances. Without the enforced regulation of desegregation court orders or guidelines designed to attain racial diversity, the implementation of uncontrolled school choice plans tends to foster racially homogeneous schools and leads to even greater racial disparities. As noted previously, this has been the case with magnet schools; and it also results in other dominant permutations of parental choice models.

Several studies reveal similar trends. For example, one study of the 22 largest US school districts found that, on average, schools were more segregated than the neighborhoods they served and that (with notable exceptions) the availability of charter, magnet, private, or other specialty schools led to even greater disparities (Saporito & Sohoni, 2006). Choice tends to exacerbate racial imbalances. The only notable exceptions were districts that operated racial desegregation programs that controlled choice options or that provided incentives sufficient to overcome racial preferences (e.g., highly effective and well-situated magnet schools). Other studies of districts that use choice or magnet schools report similar findings (Koedel, Betts, Rice, & Zau, 2009), with reviews concluding that regulated choice programs have the potential to increase the integration of schools and, at the very least, to prevent further social stratification (Cobb & Glass, 2009). As previously noted, however, these schools can increase integration, but the increases do tend to be modest.

That some programs eventually produce, at best, modest reductions in racial disparities does not necessarily mean that they should be endorsed. Research does indicate that uncontrolled choice plans lead to greater disparity and that controlled choice plans can reduce some disparities; but studies do not offer an assurance that they will do so. Also important, research examining the sorting of students under charter school programs reveals that they tend to intensify the isolation of disadvantaged students in less effective urban schools serving a high concentration of similarly disadvantaged students. Choice law may have offered hope in that just because it is not expressly designed to further integration, the belief was that it still could further integration and diversity. However, the result often has been increased segregation (Frankenberg & Lee, 2003; Hochschild & Scovronick, 2003; Horn & Miron, 2000; Howe, Eisenhart, & Betebenner, 2001). To exacerbate matters, students with fewer options are left behind, and their disadvantage increases (Ni, 2012). Whether choice and other related alternatives reach effectiveness depends on the specific circumstances of communities and individuals within them.

Uncontrolled choice plans fail to achieve or maintain racial diversity for a number of reasons. The concept of choice assumes equal access to information and similar effectiveness in taking steps needed to exercise hoped for choices. However, not all parents have access to the same kind or quality of information about new schools or existing schools. Because of the unequal distribution of information on the comparative value of different educational options, unrestricted choice plans tend to advantage parents with high educational attainment or more networks and contacts. These parents more likely benefit from choice plans compared to other parents who lack informational advantages about the available range of choices and know to exercise their options. Because White parents, on average, have more education and connection to higher-status networks, the difference between those who can choose and those who likely cannot further stratifies schools on the basis of race.

Lack of information and the ability to use available information effectively relate to other key reasons that uncontrolled school choice can exacerbate racial disparities in schooling. How economic status may not be an effective proxy for enhancing diversity in school assignments has already been discussed. That ineffectiveness mainly was due to how its effect was muted by limited variations in neighborhoods and districts. Such factors appear to work differently in school choice programs. The socioeconomic variation that may exist and relate to racial/ethnic status may exacerbate racial disparities in uncontrolled choice programs.

Socioeconomic factors can further limit the actual choices that families have when selecting schools. Notably, lack of transportation for students to attend the schools of their choice hampers its ability to enhance diversity. This point is of significance in that housing patterns account for the bulk of school segregation (Rivkin, 1994). A limited number of students from neighborhoods could have the means to benefit from choice.

Economic and other social factors aside, individual factors also limit the effectiveness of choice programs in fostering diversity. Most notably, preferences relating to race itself factor into parents' determinations of their children's school choices. A recent thorough review (Smrekar & Honey, 2015) found that school-choice studies, including those focused on intradistrict high schools (Saporito & Lareau, 1999), charter schools (Weiher & Tedin, 2002), vouchers (Schneider & Buckley, 2002), and interdistrict elementary schools (Glazerman, 1997), determined that race and class dominated parents' choice patterns. All of these studies pointed to parents' tendency to choose schools that are academically sound (using tangible measures such as test scores and perceptions of teacher quality and safety) and that reflect their race in the student majority (using available demographic information). In one case, the majority of White families (but not Black families) in the choice program followed a two-tier process, first apparently deleting majority Black schools from their choice list and then applying rules of academic quality and school safety to make a decision (Saporito & Lareau, 1999). As a result of these dynamics, many schools relying on unrestricted choice plans segregate by race and socioeconomic status.

Recent developments in this area of law increase the likelihood that racial imbalances will remain the trend. If attention to race is important to ensure that choices do not increase racial imbalances in school assignments, then addressing the resulting imbalances is no longer likely. *Parents Involved* (2007) now makes clear that the legal system largely forbids official attention to the racial composition of schools even as part of a voluntary choice plan: Neither public nor private schools can take into account the race of individual students in school assignments, except as a remedy for judicially determined racial discrimination by government actors. This means that the Court now rejects a major reason for some of these programs: It rejects voluntary efforts to address racial imbalances. That limitation makes it difficult to develop and evaluate policies that use race as an aspect of diversity.

Geographic Indicators

Rather than rely on the race of individual students to decrease racial imbalances, schools can focus on broad group indicators that evaluate each applicant as an individual and not in a way that makes an applicant's race or ethnicity the defining feature of his or her application. Following *Parents Involved*, for example, Kentucky's Jefferson County Public Schools, one of the nation's largest school districts, revised its policy by using three geographic factors to devise new attendance zones: median household income, the percentage of non-White students, and the average educational attainment of adults (Powell & Menendian, 2014). The school board sought to comply with the Supreme Court's ruling by not using individual racial classifications. Other districts have followed suit and developed similar multifactor approaches. The Berkeley Unified School District implemented a plan that manages parental choice for elementary schools using a similar diversity index that calculates the percentage of students of color, parental income level, and parental education. In addition to being prompted by the legal requirement, the idea of using multiple indicators in the construction of attendance zones emerged from research suggesting a relationship between geographic indicators and educational opportunity.

Admissions plans have become increasingly complex in terms of number and sophistication of considered factors. That complexity suggests the relative difficulty of promoting racial diversity without resorting to individual racial classifications, let alone race at the neighborhood level. Also, available evidence indicates that they may not be as effective as programs based on the individualized consideration of race. Other plans modeled on the Jefferson plan have not yet been in operation long enough to be fairly evaluated (Powell & Menendian, 2014). So far, these efforts, although maintaining some level of diversity, generally have not proved as successful as those that use individuals' race.

The reason for the reduced effectiveness in addressing racial imbalances and lack of expected findings is self-evident. Although race-neutral factors may correlate to race, they are necessarily less precise than race itself. This is true for geographical factors. The use of race at the neighborhood level may help compensate for the deficiencies in socioeconomic considerations alone because socioeconomic status is an imprecise channeling mechanism for producing a diverse student body. For example, some White students residing in hypersegregated and predominantly non-White neighborhoods are likely to be channeled through the consideration of neighborhood demographics that would otherwise not be reassigned under a more direct assignment policy. In addition, complex plans can confuse families who need to understand their operation and may increase the distance that students must travel to school. Furthermore, race-neutral plans may fail to address the multifaceted challenges that plague minority communities. Compensating for these deficiencies requires more than increasing precision. Although approximating race, these approaches are far more complex and resource intensive than using a simple race criterion, require additional expertise or outside consultants, and raise concerns about their actual effectiveness.

In addition to focusing on results that support benign effects, it is important to consider those that indicate the opposite. For example, a recent study used geospatial techniques to assess the impact of school attendance zone "gerrymandering" on the racial/ethnic segregation of schools; the study included a large national sample of 15,290 attendance zones in 663 districts (Richards, 2014). It estimated the effect of gerrymandering on school diversity and school district segregation by comparing the racial/ethnic characteristics of existing attendance zones to those of counterfactual zones expected in the absence of gerrymandering. The findings indicate that the gerrymandering of attendance zones generally exacerbates segregation, although it has a weaker effect on the segregation of Whites from Blacks and Hispanics. Gerrymandering appears particularly segregative in districts experiencing rapid racial/ethnic change. However, gerrymandering still associates with reductions in segregation in a substantial minority of districts, notably those under desegregation orders.

The previous findings reveal the challenges of using voluntary, race-neutral alternatives. Given the Court's vagueness in stating what it will expect from schools, it remains to be determined whether these alternatives are too ineffective to warrant the use of race-conscious approaches. What remains clear, however, is the need for empirical research.

The Inherent Limitations of Using Empirical Findings

The racial imbalances found throughout society result from dozens of demographic, social, and economic factors that vary across geographic areas and local conditions. The convergence of these factors with race makes race a particularly useful consideration in understanding life's chances, but this clustering also raises the challenge of untangling and analyzing the various factors that explain what constitutes one's "race." Research may guide the understanding of the number of factors that contribute to racial imbalances and the complexity of their interaction, but school assignment policies may not easily capture their cumulative effect on educational opportunity and other goals associated with encouraging diversity. In addition, research may identify root causes of disparities, but those do not lend themselves to easy solutions. For example, states and metropolitan areas with more fragmented and small district structures exhibit higher levels of what researchers view as "segregation" (Ayscue & Orfield, 2015). Although administrative needs encourage viewing race as the sum of its parts, this approach ignores the relationships between the parts. It also ignores the emergent properties of complex systems that result and constitute race itself. Diversity involves much more than simple racial categories; it involves diversity within those categories.

The challenges of finding strong and useful effects for proxies raise the critical point of how much of an effect is needed. If a large effect is needed to achieve the compelling state interest, then proxies do not suffice. Also, if the effect needs to be as great as it would be for race-conscious plans, then the use of proxies remains insufficient. On the other hand, if the principle is to ensure that other factors come into play and that those factors are important to ensuring equality, then proxies may play an important role in achieving equality. The question of whether a race-neutral alternative would perform "about as well and at tolerable administrative expense" (*Fisher I*, 2013, p. 2420) is critical, as the efficacy of alternatives has borne out. The administrative expense of developing race-neutral plans goes far beyond the resources of most admissions committees, let alone school boards and administrative staff, compared to the cost of using racial classifications in either student assignment or admissions review. These challenges are exacerbated by typical changes in communities adapting to demographic shifts. The end result is that these methods generally lack effectiveness, may be more costly, may need constant adjustment, and likely will never become effective if schools must demonstrate a high concordance. Last, the very fact that these proxies are used to replace the use of race creates a paradox; proxies would not be used were it not for racial imbalances—they exist because they address racial issues that the legal system seeks to avoid addressing explicitly.

Requiring the Minimal Necessary Use of Racial Classifications

Legally, if a court determines that a compelling interest exists to make use of racial categories to increase diversity, and if it affirms that the government sufficiently considered alternatives, then the court considers what exactly constitutes the needed diversity to achieve the ends deemed compelling. This consideration raises complex questions, some of which can be understood in empirical ways. Again, the three leading cases in this area are instructive because they address issues about the level of needed diversity. Although post-secondary level cases do remain suggestive rather than controlling decisions, they indicate what the Court would consider at primary and secondary levels if it accepted governmental assertions about the need to treat groups differently by race.

What the Law Requires

Parents Involved provides two useful starting points. The first starting point involves the need for race-conscious policies to carefully select numerical goals. Justice Roberts found the school assignment plans not narrowly tailored because they were not tied to "any pedagogic concept of the level of diversity needed to obtain the asserted educational benefits" (*Parents Involved*, 2007, p. 726). The failure to articulate the level of diversity needed, as well as the link to the reasons for diversity, proved fatal to the policy. However, the Court continued as it pointed to the school districts' use of numerical goals based on the racial composition of the general school population, and it faulted the districts for failing to prove that no other set of numbers will work. *Parents Involved* provides the lesson that the Court will require close links between the asserted need for diversity and the amount of diversity needed.

The second starting point offered by *Parents Involved* relates to the significance of the effects produced by the policies in achieving goals. Disagreement among the justices reveals the challenge. In his dissenting opinion, Justice Breyer viewed the race-conscious plans as narrowly tailored because, when used, they often had no effect because the particular school was not oversubscribed in the year in question, the racial makeup of the school fell within the broad range, or the student was a transfer applicant or had a sibling at the school. In these respects, the broad ranges were deemed less like a quota and more like useful starting points. Justice Roberts responded that such minimal effects indicate the need to reject the policy.

He observed that when considering the actual racial composition of schools, enrolling students without regard for their race yields a substantially diverse student body under any definition of diversity. As a result, he reasoned that the minimal effect that these classifications have on student assignments suggests that other means would effectively achieve diversity. Policies' minimal effects, it turns out, could be a sign of either effectiveness or ineffectiveness.

The previous starting points highlight two major questions that policies need to address: What critical mass is needed to reach asserted diversity goals? and Who has the discretion to determine that level and whether it is being reached effectively? To address these two questions, *Grutter* and the *Fisher* cases are again illustrative.

Under *Grutter*, the Court recognizes the need to articulate clearly the boundaries and rationales for the type of diversity sought by a particular policy. In that case, the Court held that the law school could permissibly seek an *unspecified* "critical mass" of students of underrepresented groups—a concept "defined by reference to the educational benefits that diversity is designed to produce"—as part of its efforts to achieve student body diversity (*Grutter v. Bollinger*, 2003, p. 330). The Court recognized the need for a critical mass to dispel stereotypes about minorities, including assumptions that minorities share the same characteristic viewpoints, and to ensure the presence of enough members of underrepresented minority groups for those students to participate in the classroom without feeling isolated or feeling like spokespersons for their race (*Id.*, pp. 318–319).

In addressing issues of critical mass, the *Fisher I* Court (pp. 2013, 2418) noted that a university is not permitted to define diversity as "some specified percentage of a particular group merely because of its race or ethnic origin." Doing so "would amount to outright racial balancing, which is patently unconstitutional" (*Id.*). The Court continued as it quoted *Parents Involved* for the admonition that "racial balancing is not transformed from 'patently unconstitutional' to a compelling state interest simply by relabeling it 'racial diversity'" (*Parents Involved*, 2007, p. 732; *Fisher I*, 2013, p. 2419). The Court further continued by noting that it approved the *Grutter* plan after concluding that it was not a quota, was sufficiently flexible, was limited in time, and followed "serious, good faith consideration of workable race-neutral alternatives" (*Fisher I*, 2013, p. 2420).

Although the Texas program was modeled after the approved Michigan program, there were important differences. Under the Texas program, an applicant is admitted based on a combination of an Academic Index (AI) and Personal Achievement Index (PAI) scores, with "race" added to the eventual number assigned to each applicant's PAI score. Once applications have been scored, they are plotted on a grid, with the AI score on the x-axis and the PAI score on the y-axis. On that grid, applicants are assigned to cells based on their individual scores. All applicants in the cells falling above a certain line are admitted. All applicants below that line are not. This approach clearly makes race matter. This approach also differs from the language and approach taken by Michigan Law School's policy. The language included both a broad conception of diversity not limited to race and ethnicity and a special emphasis on racial and ethnic diversity. The policy thus acknowledged many possible bases for diversity admissions, and it allowed substantial weight to be given in the admissions process to a wide array of experiences and backgrounds. However, at the same time, the policy reaffirmed and entrenched Michigan Law School's commitment to the enrollment of a "critical mass" of racial or ethnic minority students. Unlike Texas, there were no automatic cutoff lines; Michigan did not enumerate what constituted a critical mass. Given that neither the *Fisher I* nor the *Fisher II* Court ruled specifically on the Texas policy, it is unclear whether it is close enough to that of Michigan.

Fisher I also revealed the research used to determine the need for a critical mass. The plan to resume race-conscious admissions substantially relied on a study of a subset of undergraduate classes containing between 5 and 24 students. Few of these classes had significant enrollment by members of racial minorities. In addition, the study relied on what it called anecdotal reports from students regarding their interaction in the classroom. The study concluded that the university lacked a "critical mass" of minority students and that remedying the deficiency necessitated explicit consideration of race in the undergraduate admissions program. Given the complex issues that this area of research needs to address, the study was rudimentary at best.

The Court found debatable whether Texas could have offered evidence that would meet the Court's standards. It was debatable because the lower court had confined its strict scrutiny inquiry in too narrow a way by deferring to the university's good faith in its use of racial classifications. The Supreme Court concluded by noting that the reviewing court must assess whether the university has offered sufficient evidence proving that its admissions program is narrowly tailored to obtain the educational benefits of diversity. Without more analysis, the university's study was insufficient to support its program.

In ruling that Texas had not provided enough evidence and that the reviewing court failed to give a thorough vetting, the *Fisher I* Court emphasizes at least one key point: The government must show not only the need for diversity but also how it appropriately reaches the benefits of diversity. The government must demonstrate that it reaches those benefits in a way that infringes the least on the rights of others not to be treated differently—in this case, not being disadvantaged by not gaining admission to the university—because of their racial status. As is the case with other aspects of this area of study, the Court requires the government to reach a very tricky standard—one that is needed yet potentially fatal to the government's goals. Still, the heightened standard of review is not impossible to reach. When the Supreme Court revisited *Fisher I*, the majority concluded that the university had met its burden of showing that its policy was narrowly tailored—that the university's policies appropriately reached its educational goals and that no alternative, workable means had been proffered in the course of the litigation.

Together, *Grutter* and the *Fisher* cases reveal at least one important lesson: Individualized determinations using race will be submitted to strict scrutiny. *Grutter*, at least in the university admissions context, jettisoned the "minimum necessary preference" requirement and replaced it with a requirement that affirmative action programs be "individualized"—that race is one factor among others used in a holistic manner. *Gratz*, *Grutter's* companion case, had rejected the use of race because it had not been individualized. *Grutter* had not mechanically added predetermined points to every minority applicant. As a result, the approach develops a regime of do not tell, will not ask: If the government decision maker does not "tell" courts how much of a racial preference it is giving (by not quantifying its preferences), courts will essentially not "ask" probing questions about whether the preferences are differentiated or excessive. *Fisher I* (2013) apparently had put an end to the high deference. Texas' program mimicked *Grutter's* because it used a holistic approach that included race. The major difference in the cases was that the lower courts in *Fisher I* had not sufficiently scrutinized the school's decisions. *Fisher I* had confirmed that the Court will submit plans reporting individualized determinations using race to strict scrutiny. *Fisher I's* refusal to leave broad discretion to schools requires them to be explicit, which brings close scrutiny. However, in the follow-up case, *Fisher II* (2016), the Court still supported the program because the enhanced scrutiny revealed it to be justified. It was justified even though the university would not reveal how relevant race actually was to the holistic decisions. The point that emerges is that if race matters, then strict scrutiny follows it; also, if race matters, then the Court may allow its use even under considerable uncertainty about the nature and extent of that use.

Empirical Challenges and Findings

Efforts to determine the level of diversity needed to achieve compelling interests in narrowly tailored ways face fundamental challenges. As currently understood, this area of law raises two broad issues to address empirically. The first relates to the Court's apparent openness, for primary and secondary schools, to ensuring a "critical mass" of individuals who fall into particular categories to achieve asserted compelling interests. The second relates to the relevance of empirical research in achieving diversity's goals through individualized considerations rather than approaches requiring a preset critical mass. Both of these approaches create challenges.

Determining Critical Mass

The Court's openness to reaching diversity needed for a critical mass remains limited by practical challenges. The first challenge is that the potential interest in diversity (beyond remedying de jure discrimination) has been accepted for university-level admissions, not necessarily primary and secondary schools. The second is that if accepted for primary and secondary schools, challenges abound because a myriad of types of interests could be at stake and the nature of communities varies.

The challenges are obvious in efforts to determine critical mass for the goal of achieving intellectual diversity, the most widely accepted goal for post-secondary education. How much diversity is needed to reach intended outcomes remains both unclear and indeterminate. Policies cannot be considered to be narrowly tailored to achieve the type of free speech needed for intellectual diversity. It would be difficult, if not impossible, to make the connection that using race in student selections is an essential and precisely crafted mechanism to ensuring a multiplicity of ideas in classrooms.

In addition to not reaching particular goals, the use of race itself may be problematic. Using race to determine whether individuals will bring experiences and express them in school environments essentializes race. It assumes that persons of a given race will have given experiences, express given viewpoints, or have given ideas. To exacerbate matters, such determinations become mind-boggling in the context of multiethnic communities. The concepts of ethnicity and race are contested; individuals need not view themselves as belonging to a group that some would ascribe to them, and they themselves can be multiethnic. In fact, research has tended to ignore the contested nature of race, as has the legal system.

Assumptions of race also create challenges because policies may not use quotas or seek proportional representation. For example, the Court has ruled against separate admission tracks for applicants of different races and insulation of applicants from competition with the entire pool (*Grutter v. Bollinger*, 2003, pp. 333–334; *Regents of the University of California v. Bakke*, 1978, p. 314). This critique may seem to be an overly narrow one, but the nature of ethnicity and race, and what those categories mean, continues to change and is not as easily identifiable as once thought because ethnicity itself is marked by much diversity.

Rather than focus on goals of diversity, the focus could be on group balancing and ensuring that it is appropriately maintained. The dissenting opinion in *Parents Involved* pointed to research-based evidence supporting, for example, that a ratio no greater than 50 percent minority is helpful in limiting the risk of White flight. The 50-percent point also has the benefit of already being recognized in law. For example, federal law assumes that a similar target percentage will help avoid detrimental minority group isolation; see No Child Left Behind Act of 2001, Title V, Part C, 115 Stat. 1806, 20 U. S. C. §7231 et seq. (2000 ed., Supp. IV); 34 CFR §§280.2, 280.4 (2006) (implementing regulations). These figures have been offered as reasonable starting points.

The 50-percent tipping point may appear reasonable, but it has been disputed. Evidence relating to White flight has centered on determining statistical tipping points. Whether desegregation leads to White flight has been controversial (Pettigrew & Green, 1976). The controversy has not suffered from a lack of empirical research. It started with groundbreaking findings by Coleman (1975) indicating that integration plans accelerate White flight, especially in the presence of surrounding predominantly White suburbs. That research was subsequently debated (Armor, 1980; Pettigrew & Green, 1976). For the most part, scholars now recognize a general trend of Whites moving away from urban centers, but this movement is accelerated by the presence of a desegregation order. Rather than 50 percent, some researchers have identified some tipping points to be in the 20–30 percent range (Farley, Schuman, Bianchi, Colasanto, & Hatchett, 1978). As expected, much depends on what is being measured. In addition, given that diversity is being sought in other ways than desegregation orders, research now is less useful. The overall conclusion that emerges, however, is that the dynamics of racial compositions tend to be nonlinear; intergroup dynamics often appear to be dramatically affected at specific racial ratios. Tipping points can vary depending on multiple factors (Davis, Strube, & Cheng, 1995).

Despite broad consensus regarding the effect of desegregation orders on White flight, debate continues over the magnitude of the effect. Now, a variety of school choices can come into play without having students move out of a district. Concern about equal influx and outflux does not capture the needed nuances of balancing. This is important because concerns about tipping points typically refer to the point at which an influx of Blacks under a desegregation order causes a comparable outflux of Whites. The magnitude of the effect is important to consider so that courts may fashion remedies tailored to avoid the possible neutralizing effects that White flight from particular schools or programs might otherwise have on efforts to achieve diversity.

The leading study in this area has been Clotfelter's (1976) examination of the role of school racial composition in the demand for private schooling by Whites. Using a sample of US metropolitan areas in 1960 and 1970, he found that an increase in the proportion of minorities in public schools of 10 percent associates with an increase in the proportion of Whites in private schools of 1–8 percent. Recent research reveals that a 1-percentage-point increase in the county (metropolitan area) level minority share of school-age population increases the private schooling probability of White students by 0.2 (0.27) percentage points (Li, 2009). Although it may be difficult to understand the relevance of these figures to specific situations, they do indicate that efforts to achieve diversity have consequences for parents' actions: Increasing the presence of one group affects the presence of another group.

Putting aside challenges of determining tipping points and which tipping points matter, research addressing critical mass issues also has focused on the harms of tokenism and stereotype threat that arise in the contexts of racial isolation (insufficient numbers of a minority group). For example, research has long shown that token numbers of students expose students to harassment from peers and constrict the possibility of increasing the necessary interactions and contact necessary for the reduction of prejudice (Allport, 1954). For example, Schofield and Sagar (1983) found that self-segregation occurs when the group is less than 15 percent of the student body to the extent that they are more likely to choose friends on the basis of group membership. Another researcher concluded that approximately equal proportions are best for maximizing intergroup friendships (McConahay, 1981). On the other hand, research also indicates that integrated schools and classrooms may experience higher levels of racial and ethnic tension and hence produce fewer positive interracial relationships than environments with relatively small minority populations (see, e.g., research on victimization: Hanish & Guerra, 2000; Vervoort, Scholte, & Overbeek, 2010).

The diverse findings may be attributable to many causes, but a likely reason is that critical mass remains an amorphous concept and much depends on how schools structure themselves to allow interactions. Any specific percentage of a group does not guarantee positive relationships or other specific outcomes, as positive outcomes derive from appropriately structured school environments. Not surprisingly, when it analyzed the authorities cited in amicus briefs supporting the use of race-conscious policies, the National Academy of Education (Linn & Welner, 2007) concluded that evidence was insufficiently strong to support any firm percentage for creating a critical mass.

A close examination of research relating to "critical mass" justifications for race-conscious policies reveals three key points. First, research remains inadequate to determine what would constitute a critical mass for the purposes of reaching diversity's goals in primary and secondary schools. Second, existing research supporting a particular critical mass metric would not pass the strict scrutiny test because the empirical data simply do not support a particular position and existing findings reveal complexities difficult to put into practice. Third, even if relevant research did exist, available research would not substitute for a specific program's evaluation, which would have to reflect each institution's specific needs. This is unlikely to happen given that a school would need a program in place to evaluate it and given that the school must prove a need for the program in order to have it. Arguing that a policy is used only to the minimum extent necessary to achieve goals makes for a rather difficult task.

Deferring to Schools' Views of Critical Mass

Given the inherent problems with critical mass issues, a way to address them is to ignore them, which is precisely what the Court has permitted in the post-secondary context (*Fisher II*, 2016). The Court can leave these issues to the discretion of decision makers. This approach poses several challenges to empirical analyses.

Determining the place of empirical analyses in discretionary regimes becomes challenging because they could be irrelevant. For example, the Court's preference for unquantified plans makes it difficult to perform any kind of cost–benefit calculus. This difficulty is odd because quantification is necessary to determine whether a preference is the minimum necessary. Some sort of quantification would be a necessary prerequisite to test whether racial preferences are narrowly tailored to achieve the government's compelling interest. Moving away from the minimum necessary preference standard, the Court does not require universities to quantify the costs and benefits of their affirmative action programs. It requires that analysis, and submits it to strict scrutiny, when the universities do reveal that they consider racial status. Simply stated, only overt quantifying requires close empirical analysis.

Discretionary regimes raise other problems for empirical analyses. A legal rule that leaves discretion to decision makers may be evaluated empirically to determine whether it is an effective rule that reaches its objectives. It can only be evaluated, however, if evidence is available and transparent. This is a fundamental problem with discretion. Justice Ginsburg recognized the problem in her dissenting opinion in *Gratz*. In it, she chides the Court for preferring the "winks" and "nods" inherent in the amorphous standards of individualized consideration (*Gratz v. Bollinger*, 2003, p. 305). An individualized model makes it impossible for anyone outside an admissions committee to determine how much weight they give to race generally or to particular racial subgroups. Even admissions officers may not be able to determine how much weight they give to race (*Fisher II*, 2016), which results in making no effort to address how individual characteristics of students admitted under race-conscious systems would have not been permissible under race-neutral systems. This is unlike a critical mass approach in which the government's decision maker pre-commits to a particular weight applied evenly across the board. Although the outcome of particular discretionary regimes could be examined, those results would be difficult to interpret if they are derived from discretion that can weigh multiple factors.

Research reveals that the other fundamental problem with individualized discretionary approaches involves discrimination. Individualized consideration gives state actors the power not just to notice race but also to define race, on a case-by-case basis. This power makes race more relevant to some applicants than to others. Research reveals that this approach is problematic for at least two reasons. Such power creates a stereotyping danger. By permitting discretion to decide "who counts," individualized consideration opens the door to stereotypical decision-making because it gives schools the power to determine which applicants' races or ethnicities will contribute to the representation of those races or ethnicities. The second danger is reverse covering: Individualized consideration requires people to perform their ethnicity for schools, such as through their personal statements or entrance interviews. It raises the problem that the government pressures individuals to behave in ways that conform to and signal their group status and how they (stereotypically) are different from the dominant culture. Legally, this is problematic because it makes race important in government decisions when the government is supposed to avoid it. It particularly is difficult in this situation because individuals are supposed to self-define and not face governmental pressure to identify with particular groups. Having individuals make commitments to racial identities that the government then uses for differential treatment ensures that race will continue to be part of governmental decisions—a policy approach that the Court itself deems illegitimate.

The Court has offered a way to deal with quota issues that, even if deemed legitimate, also raises concerns. Requiring race-conscious policies to focus on race as one factor in the decision-making process, and not overtly specifying how it is being used, makes important assumptions about race. Fundamentally, it assumes that race can be identified. Although race may be an overt and obvious marker in everyday life, it becomes much less one when part of governmental classifications. In fact, researchers have revealed how general policies meant to benefit members of a race are inadequate given diversity within racial groups (Brown, 2014). The failure to reach goals has much to do with announced goals, methods of reaching them, and situational dynamics. Enhancing diversity itself may not address the fundamental reasons for addressing diversity given the diversity of groups. Addressing these concerns requires clear legal standards, rationales, and transparency that can support useful evaluations. This has been what judicial scrutiny is all about—to evaluate specific situations and guide responses for others.

Conclusions

An often ignored area of research needed to address governmental efforts to treat people differently by using racial classifications involves the necessity to evaluate remedial approaches as well as potential alternatives. These are important analyses due to the manner in which the Supreme Court has developed its doctrine relating to treating protected group markers, such as race, similarly or differently. Given that current jurisprudence pronounces the government's use of protected categories as inherently suspect, efforts to use them, such as through race-conscious policies, must demonstrate serious consideration of neutral means to reach the articulated compelling interests. This consideration is necessary in that effective alternatives are preferable to making group classifications. As a result, the government must consider alternatives even though it could be shown that race-conscious policies do help achieve intended goals. Even if evidence would support the compelling interests supporting the use of race-conscious mechanisms, the legal system still requires that they be furthered in a narrowly tailored manner that would make them both necessary and least infringing on others' protected rights.

The conclusion that emerges from empirical research determining whether to permit race-conscious polices and evaluate their effects reveals that, although they may play a role in shaping efforts, empirical findings currently remain quite limited. Existing empirical evidence does not appear strong enough to challenge the increasingly entrenched view that the Constitution's "equal protection of laws" mandate bars supporting differential treatment to increase opportunities. Nor does it support differential treatment to reach equal ends given how the legal system approaches segregation and the related experiences of discrimination, prejudice, and disparities in treatment. The consideration of neutral alternatives and ensuring minimal infringement on everyone's right to be treated equally regardless of their race—twin requirements for the proper implementation of race-conscious efforts—create important empirical challenges. The legal system frames legal questions in ways that appear amenable to empirical evaluation. But, so far, the empirical record does not strongly support legal assumptions, and the legal system makes it difficult to produce needed findings.

6

Lessons from the Law and Empirical Research Addressing School Segregation and Diversity

Unnecessary Gaps Between Law and Empirical Research

Supreme Court doctrine can be squirrelly. The Court can bar actions only to eventually find them permissible. And it even can do the opposite: make something permissible only to find it impermissible a few years later. Even when it settles issues, the result can be so contentious that it leaves matters unsettled; or unanimous agreement can be so narrow or vague that it fails to guide its application to other situations. As a result, much can remain ambivalent and unsettled. The legal system can act this way because it defines the contours of issues and determines its own ways of approaching them.

The previous characterization of the legal system may seem unfair and unfamiliar. But it describes how the legal system has addressed school segregation and racial disparities in the composition of schools and opportunities they provide. The most obvious example is the Court's historical embrace of segregation, then its rejection of it, and now its adoption of a neutral stance toward most racial disparities in schooling. Perhaps even more telling of the ambivalence is the extent to which commentators and justices take different positions on these issues: They even disagree about whether their stances are contradictory and faithful to established legal principles.

Much of the ambivalence in this area of law actually is quite subtle. For example, the Court now requires post-secondary schools to meet very high standards before adopting race-conscious policies to address disparities in educational access. However, such high standards may be pointless because the Court leaves key interpretations to the discretion of those who created or implemented the policies (*Fisher II: Fisher v. the University of Texas*, 2016). As yet another example, the University of Michigan Law School's affirmative action case affirmed, for the first time in a majority opinion, the principle that the government has a compelling interest to support diversity (*Grutter v. Bollinger*, 2003). That affirmation ambivalently leaves the use of racial classifications both as something inherently suspect to be rejected and as something positive and allowable as a "plus" factor to ensure diversity. Furthermore, the Court never has convincingly revealed why it has rejected the diversity argument in the contexts of primary and secondary schools (*Parents Involved in Community Schools v. Seattle School District No. 1*, 2007). All of the contemporary leading cases reflect considerable ambivalence and contradictions.

The legal system tends to be unbothered by the appearance of contradictory, ambivalent, or unsettled positions. The different positions emerge from deeply held principles and precedents that have served the legal system well enough. The legal system can make due with Supreme Court cases built on slim majorities and forceful dissenting views. However, the legal system's approach raises concerns, not the least of which is how different legal positions can foster ineffective policies and leave gaping disparities in individuals' life circumstances and opportunities.

This book concerned itself with the gap between legal positions and their effectiveness in addressing segregation and its apparent harms, including the failure to benefit from diversity. The examination revealed that the legal system's now dominant focus on neutrality toward different racial and ethnic groups masks complexities and leaves room for discretion and biases. In turn, those complexities reveal how the legal system reflects societal acquiescence and that such acquiescence can be reframed to develop the legal principles that animated the legal system's need to assert itself in the first instance. The reframing can be achieved through more effective use of empirical findings. Empirical understandings of the legal system can reinforce the system's efforts to reach its announced goals, particularly goals involving equal opportunity and fair treatment. This view directly challenges the emerging dominant belief that the legal system has little use for empirical findings and that this area of law must forbid efforts that more deliberately address disparities. Overall, these lessons reveal the importance of understanding the legal system's needs and how those understandings serve as key starting points. A look at the legal system's use of empirical research reveals that its needs should remain just that—starting points.

Legal Rules Cannot Be Ignored

Researchers pervasively ignore basic legal rules, and they do so at their own peril. Whether a legal matter "exists" is a product of how the legal system chooses to define and address it. As much as researchers may document discrimination or segregation as problematic, it becomes legally problematic only when the legal system recognizes it as such. In addition, as the dominant controlling system in society, the legal system determines much of what society can do to address its problems; it even shapes the nature of envisioned alternatives. The legal system's power to define and limit alternative visions of what matters poses a fundamental problem for empirical research: Researchers have often ineffectively responded to both what the legal system requests and what the legal system could use to address matters differently.

Empirical analyses of segregation and its related constructs frequently ignore or fail to reflect an understanding of legal needs. The use of the term "segregation" by researchers who focus on racial imbalances in schools provides the clearest example. Even the most recent reviews of research relating to racial imbalances refer to them as segregation (Reardon & Owens, 2014). However, they describe a situation that the legal system does not recognize as segregation. What researchers describe may include segregating situations, but the disparities generally do not qualify as segregation because the legal system did not directly create them by distinguishing people on the basis of race. In fact, the legal system does not even deem the described situations as inappropriate or in need of redressing; the system even bars direct efforts to address them.

Researchers' use of the term "discrimination" also illustrates the failure to recognize the law's needs. Recent research on discrimination during adolescence, for example, simply asks participants about their experiences of being treated differently due to their race, ethnicity, gender, sexual orientation, or other group status of interest to researchers. These studies generally fail to denote the actual sources of discrimination. Although that research may be important for many empirical reasons, it lacks legal relevance because it misses the point that sources of discriminatory actions matter in law. Private prejudices generally fall outside of legal concerns. This is particularly true in the context of public schools. The discrimination that matters is the school's own discrimination. As a result, researchers' labeled discrimination may be prejudicial treatment but not something directly addressable by the legal system.

The central implication of ignoring legal needs is that empirical research seeking to influence the legal system pervasively fails to do so. Researchers seeking to influence law and policy need to pay closer attention to legal definitions and approaches to the issues they study. This simple lesson may appear obvious, but researchers exhibit a remarkable tendency to ignore it. Notably, in April 2016, the US Government Accountability Office, which essentially is the research arm of Congress, issued a report titled *K–12 Education: Better Use of Information Could Help Agencies Identify Disparities and Address Racial Discrimination*. The researchers did, among other things, what researchers typically do. They failed to use legal definitions of discrimination and segregation, a failure that renders analyses irrelevant. In addition, they argued for the development of data that allow for comparing different school districts. This also was an unhelpful recommendation because litigation and desegregation efforts focus on specific cases and specific situations, which makes research from other districts irrelevant. As a result, the report was highly criticized as irrelevant by the US Department of Justice, the very agency the report was supposed to assist. Equally important, the report was not even useful for the US Department of Education. That agency could not act on findings relating to the identified disparities because the legal system currently bars it from doing so. Reports such as this exemplify the limited contribution of researchers in this area, as they repeat prior findings relating to group disparities and fail to move policy-making forward.

The tendency of research to miss the legal system's needs when addressing legal matters, however, is understandable. Many reasons account for the mismatch between legal needs and empirical research. The two dominant reasons point to the nature of the legal system's needs rather than the abilities of researchers.

The first reason why researchers often fail to develop research that could address the law's needs emerges from the manner in which the legal system can set impossible standards. For example, if the segregation that matters is the one that the law explicitly creates, then researchers likely will produce ineffective empirical research because the legal system explicitly has banned the use of race to segregate individuals. The legal system assumes that segregation in elementary and secondary schools is a thing of the past. In fact, only 178 active cases of desegregation exist (Government Accountability Office, 2016). When the legal system addresses new efforts to permit the government to use race to treat people differently, it generally does so to foster integration, not desegregation, which can only be a response to formally segregated situations. As a result, the effects and nature of segregation cannot be studied in a legally compelling way because segregation no longer exists.

The second reason for failing to provide the legal system with helpful research is that when the legal system sets standards not impossible to reach, it can make the standards too challenging. Illustrative is the call for schools to announce a needed critical mass of students from different racial groups required to assert compelling governmental interests, such as the educational benefits of diversity, to adopt race-conscious policies. Such calls are important to the legal system's evaluations of remedies. They also are intuitively appealing because they ask about the remedy's magnitude. However, the needed research reveals how the legal system fails to appreciate how what constitutes a critical mass varies from one context to the next and from one time to another as groups change. As a result, the Court's willingness to consider research may be a nod to the utility of empirical findings, but the invitation is difficult to take seriously when the legal system sets such high standards. Requiring that research meet exceedingly high standards reasonably could be viewed as a way to support a predetermined legal position or way to rely on subjective analyses that render research irrelevant. Regardless of the reasons for ignoring research, the results are the same: Researchers' general findings do not sufficiently respond to current legal needs.

Ideals of Neutrality Mask Complexities

Before placing the blame for the failure to foster appropriate research to address the legal needs on either the legal system or empirical researchers, it is important to recognize that both share similarities that hamper effective responses to social issues. Notably, the legal system and empirical research champion neutral positions. They do so even though the embrace of neutrality remains impossible in practice. This impossibility is important to consider because a focus on neutral stances masks complexities that can be counterproductive and even can create problematic situations that neutral stances were meant to attenuate. The masking of complexities particularly operates in the context of segregation law and efforts to address racial/ethnic diversity.

Neutrality in Law

Several examples illustrate how the Court's approach to racial differences increasingly rests on notions of neutrality. As currently formulated, differential treatment does not count if it occurs in the absence of direct governmental action. Without direct governmental action, racial imbalances are natural occurrences that the legal system cannot redress directly. If the government is neutral, and race is not a direct part of governmental decision-making, then unequal treatment is natural and does not result from the legal system. In fact, the government's neutrality means that differential treatment actually is not "treatment"; the government was not involved in creating the difference. This line of logic leads the Court to require the government to closely consider race-neutral alternatives before adopting race-conscious policies. Given that neutral approaches are deemed possible, they are preferred to approaches that directly take race into consideration.

As currently approached, assumptions of neutrality are problematic because they avoid considering structural conditions that exist when the government adopted the neutral position. As a result, for example, a narrow approach to neutrality ignores the influence wielded by those already in power. Doing so downplays how defining issues influences outcomes; it overlooks how political orientations influence definitions and how to address issues. In addition, it discounts the significance of history and the present-day effects of past legal rules. Illustrative is the designation of situations involving racial imbalance in the racial composition of schools as matters other than segregation; a look at racial imbalances reveals harms similar to those from segregation, but the legal system does not recognize those harms because the situations are not conceived as segregated. In essence, the legal system ignores biases influencing approaches and outcomes.

A focus on neutrality also avoids considering people's own inclinations that stifle the legal system's efforts. The legal system may want to create equality by assuming a neutral stance, but that position fails when it allows individuals to act on their own biases. Illustrative is the manner in which magnet schools can contribute to racial imbalances when they were designed to redress them. Racial considerations factor in parents' decisions when they are given the choice to send their children to particular magnet schools or to opt for other schooling options. Parents tend to prefer schools that reflect their own racial preferences, not even those of their children. The government's adopting a neutral program to address diversity becomes ineffective because it fails to consider that individuals themselves do not act neutrally. It fails to consider, in this context, how parents discriminate based on race. A neutral posture by the government foils the apparently important goal of enhancing equality.

Neutrality also is problematic when it leads to ignoring motivations. Motivations generally do not matter when laws are assumed to be neutral. They also may not matter even when the laws are meant to redress disparities. For example, Justice Ginsberg dissented in *Fisher v. the University of Texas* (*Fisher I*, 2013) to take issue with the Court's characterization of Texas' Top Ten Percent Plan as race-neutral. The plan successfully achieves its diversity goals because it draws from students who live in racially segregated housing and school districts. This means that the plan works because of the failures of earlier efforts to address housing and achieve effective desegregation. According to Justice Ginsburg, the "supposedly neutral alternatives" are driven by "race consciousness, not blindness to race" (p. 2433). Consequently, Justice Ginsburg would identify the plan for what it is: a race-conscious admissions policy that seeks to remedy past failures. She recognizes that race-neutral alternative policies would not exist unless they were motivated by addressing racially linked needs. However, she was alone in challenging the conceptualization of the law as neutral.

Neutrality also is problematic because it can become a double-edged sword. For example, the justices' labels of Texas' legislative diversity initiative create a paradox for either side of the affirmative action debate. Labeling the Top Ten Percent Plan race-conscious undermines Justice Ginsburg's goal of forthrightly addressing racial disparities. Legally, race-conscious legislation faces the almost insurmountable hurdle of strict scrutiny review. Politically, it undermines the type of consensus that a race-neutral label could garner more easily. Designating the policy as race-conscious could dismantle the diversity initiative that a majority of the Court appeared poised to uphold and eventually did (*Fisher II*, 2016). On the other hand, a race-neutral label, while guaranteeing the plan's likely constitutional approval, signals complacency and ignores some aspects of reality. Characterizing the admissions programs as neutral creates a sense that society need not undo the lingering effects of discrimination. That leads to the perplexing question of why programs remain needed if they are neutral. When laws exist to address a need, such as existing group disparities, it cannot be said to be neutral. In this instance, a system that treats 10 percent "neutrally" to address a past harm leaves the remaining 90 percent without redress; a system that fails to offer opportunities to 90 percent cannot be said to be an effective remedy for broad, group-based subjugation.

Neutrality in Empirical Evidence

The legal system's attachment to neutrality is mirrored in empirical research that has long embraced neutrality as an ideal. Science has had an uneasy relationship with politics. Much effort has been made to develop a science separate from political influences, in the sense of rendering it objective and separate from institutional structures, priorities, political parties, religious doctrine, and other conflicts of interest. However, removing empirical research from overt conflicts of interest also creates a paradoxical effect: Removing formal external influences fosters the development of a science that becomes authoritarian. The norms of neutrality and objectivity silence other ways of approaching issues; they also ignore many types of biases.

Professions of neutrality are problematic and mask distortions. They defend and legitimize the institutions and practices that generate distortions and their potential exploitative consequences. They certify as value-neutral, normal, natural, and therefore not political the rules and methods through which groups gain the information needed to advance their priorities. Such information and explanations may well "work" to explain or solve particular problems, but they are not necessarily neutral. As already seen, much scientific racism and sexism was produced by the most distinguished and, in some cases, progressive 19th-century scientists. Science is a socially embedded activity. Much development in social science does not record a closer approach to absolute truth; rather, its development reflects the alteration of cultural contexts that influence it. Its findings are snapshots of changing realities.

The strong attachment to objective, neutral science renders researchers (as well as consumers of empirical findings) less likely to recognize its problems. Sharing assumptions reduces the chances that the scientific community's careful applications of existing scientific methods will detect problems inherent in neutral stances. What could be recognized, however, is researchers' being subjected to personal and professional pressures that may distort the results of their studies. Research findings may, for example, impact a range of scientists' interests, including job security, promotion, salary, and professional prestige. Scientists also may have an interest in protecting a viewpoint endorsed in their prior work or even their colleagues' work. Bias runs through the research process in the selection of issues and research questions and also in the collection of data. Research can never be totally separated from the political, personal, and professional opinions of those creating it.

Several examples of empirical biases in this area are readily obvious yet pervasively ignored. Perhaps the exemplar of biased research is the persistent focus on highlighting group disparities as well as group differences. This strong attachment to revealing group imbalances and situations that appear unfair, for example, ignores that the legal system needs specificity in identifying the sources of the imbalances and unfairness. The same is true for research highlighting prejudicial treatment. Research is replete with findings indicating a wide variety of reasons why individuals exhibit prejudice toward a wide variety of personal characteristics. And researchers also may document well the pernicious outcomes of these prejudices. Researchers even may broadly agree about identified harms. However, such research runs the risk of being legally irrelevant because only some harms gain the law's protection and can secure legal responses.

Just like judicial bias, researchers' biases may follow cultural or ideological bias that may distort empirical findings. Researcher bias may be particularly strong in studies that have implications for controversial public policy questions, such as those addressing diversity. For example, beliefs about causation closely tie to beliefs about desirable effects. A view of racial integration as undesirable frequently accompanies a view that individual merit plays a key role in causing society's current segregation. Contrariwise, viewing racial integration as desirable accompanies the view that social segregation results from forces other than individual merit. These different roles given to individual merit has consequences. Perceptions of individual merit influence interpretations of diversity, even when it is unclear what role individual merit does or should play in addressing diversity.

As an example of the previously mentioned biases, the Top Ten Percent Plan and its modifications embraced by Texas employ a group remedy to address the vestiges of group subjugation. The approach is particularly important because it remains the only approved race-conscious approach outside of desegregation contexts. As such, it likely could serve as a model for enhancing diversity in primary and secondary school levels. However, the remedy actually ignores the vast majority of students who do not qualify for preferential treatment. In a real sense, those who are most subjugated receive the least benefit from race-conscious policies. Yet, the University of Texas, following the lead of empiricist and leading educators who understand well how to interpret empirical findings, adopted the policy. Ironically, the university eventually recognized how the plan failed because it was actually creating homogeneous groups of students because the most successful students were actually quite similar, regardless of racial diversity. It was the university's response to that recognition that led to the *Fisher* cases (*Fisher I*, 2013; *Fisher II*, 2016). The Supreme Court approved. Ironically, when the Court did approve it, it did so by describing the need to give schools the power to increase diversity (*Fisher II*, 2016). In doing so, the Court focused on individual merit of particular students and ignored their relationship to their ethnic groups, even when that relationship was the reason for the challenged policy in the first place.

From an empirical perspective, the support that *Fisher II* (2016) receives from legal scholars and empiricists is ironic for even more fundamental reasons. Both groups supported the university's approach even when the university insisted that it does not and cannot keep records of the actual role that racial/ethnic characteristics played in admissions decisions. Researchers embraced an approach fundamentally at odds with basic empirical analysis, one that leaves the admissions process open to prejudice and biased decisions. Like legal commentators, they ignore that prejudice animated the reasons for the policies that sought to enhance equality. They embrace a system that rejects overt bias over one that implants opportunities ripe for the use of hidden prejudices. In the end, it may be individual merit or group status that influences individual admissions decisions. We will never know; however, we do know that it was group prejudice that the legal system sought to remedy.

It is worth repeating that empiricists have ignored the legal system's needs when examining racial and ethnic disparities. When they do address the legal system's needs, they have gone along without questioning the legal system's approach to remedying inequality, as the system has done in supporting the University of Texas' approach knowing that it is empirically problematic. Again, the problems arise not because we are dealing with complex studies; all that is needed is simple data to conduct elementary statistics.

The previous examples of biases and failures to grasp the significance of some findings illustrate the enormity of the challenge of addressing apparently neutral practices. It is only the beginning of the challenge. The detection of biases is difficult when dealing with the presentation of simple statistical findings. There is no reason to doubt that similar biases exist in more complex studies and analyses. Advanced quantitative research particularly is presented with an air of neutrality when it too is subject to assumptions and biases that shape results. Empirical studies have an uncanny ability to present themselves as containing unbiased truth.

Scrutiny Always Rests on Discretion and Biases

Concerns about the lack of neutrality in law and empirical research often lead to calls for enhanced scrutiny and a healthy sense of skepticism. The notion is that a thorough vetting of different positions, including neutral ones, can best inform the legal system. By delineating different positions, scrutiny can help focus on what the legal system does as well as what it leaves alone. However, scrutiny itself also has important limitations. Scrutiny still leaves room for discretion and use of biases. This room is seen in the different levels of scrutiny that the legal system uses to address governmental infringements on rights. As expected, the limitations of scrutiny play into the failure to address effectively the diverse manifestations of segregation and racial disparities.

We already have seen how problematic reviews of governmental actions are when they require the least scrutiny, such as when the government is being neutral. In cases involving racial disparities, close scrutiny means skepticism about "neutral" explanations for glaring disparities that cannot be explained on any other grounds except race. This scrutiny leads to critiques of neutrality in all of its permutations ranging from individual school choice to the malleable concept of diversity. The end result of that close examination may uncover unexpected findings, but it has the benefit of allowing for the type of deliberation, accommodation, and commitment deemed important when involving highly regarded rights. However, that close scrutiny itself may be ineffective if it seeks an outcome that is neutral, fair, and just for all. Policy decisions rest on using discretion and biases; they often create winners and losers.

Although it may be expected that minimal scrutiny could create problematic results, such results also can emerge from the highest levels of scrutiny. The different views expressed in *Parents Involved* (2007) illustrate how even strict scrutiny can leave much undetermined. Even strict scrutiny routinely leads to unexpected outcomes—outcomes that commentators often track along the political and jurisprudential orientations of individual Supreme Court justices.

Different perspectives of the utility and nature of strict scrutiny emerged in *Parents Involved* (2007), as the case highlighted how the closest scrutiny can be indeterminate and mask biases. Justice Breyer's dissent relied on empirical studies to argue for a compelling "educational element" in providing integrated education. Although he recognized disagreement among social scientists, he concluded that "the evidence supporting an educational interest in racially integrated schools is well established and strong enough to permit a democratically elected school board reasonably to determine that this interest is a compelling one" (*Id.*, p. 2821). By contrast, Justice Thomas' concurrence pointed to the "fervent debate" among social scientists as a reason not to defer to the decisions of elected officials" (*Id.*, p. 2773). Indeed, he saw the empirical evidence as legally irrelevant:

> We are not social engineers. The United States Constitution dictates that local governments cannot make decisions on the basis of race. Consequently, regardless of the perceived negative effects of racial imbalance, I will not defer to legislative majorities where the Constitution forbids it. (*Id.*, p. 2779)

For Justice Thomas, the dissenters' claimed deference to the democratic branches was disingenuous; he viewed their deference as the necessary result of agreeing with the school boards' assessment of the disputed empirical evidence.

The previously mentioned dispute between the justices illustrates several points. The rigor of strict scrutiny can be different for different justices who, as a result, can take different positions about the same evidence. The dispute also reveals that at some point, a decision needs to be made to resolve a dispute. Who will resolve the dispute can matter, as it could be a group of justices or it could be communities. The dispute also underscores the problematic nature of discretion and its inevitable presence. Even when the legal system adopts a rigorous standard of scrutiny, it leaves discretion and bias that will influence legal interpretations and applications.

The previous three points are heightened when dealing with segregation and racial imbalances. The entire history of discrimination law reveals an effort to align local with federal policies when schools historically have been the subject of local control. Likewise, the legal system often involves disputes between deciding issues by using case-by-case approaches and deciding them by using approaches with bright lines that reduce discretion. But the dispute is particularly troublesome in the context of discrimination. Discretion inherent in case-by-case approaches permits the use of biases and, as we have learned, even the bright line approach introduces biases that may go ignored. Last, empirical research always reveals nuances and lack of findings. Nuances in empirical findings always will exist given different methods, samples, contexts, and biases inherent in framing studies. These nuances are especially problematic in this area of law given how, depending on views of legal needs, much of the empirical research can be discounted as irrelevant, particularly when it contradicts legal positions.

The Legal System Reflects Societal Acquiescence

The inherently biased nature of legal and empirical positions may lead to a sense of futility, but that need not be the case. A critical understanding of both the legal system and empirical research reveals that the Supreme Court mirrors society at least as much as it shapes it. Blaming the Court for regressive or progressive positions does not absolve larger society of its share of responsibility for their outcomes. The Court does not embrace broad judicial principles and make specific legal rulings without society's acquiescence. Nor does it do so without researchers' acquiescence when researchers fail to address relevant legal needs or fail to properly address the legal system's own assumptions and motivations. This neglected point is important for understanding legal responses to disparities experienced by different ethnic and racial groups.

Policies that result in racial disparities lead to questioning what society really wants. For example, racial disparities in the school-to-prison pipeline are very real. So is the disparate incarceration of minority youth. So is the effect of unregulated charter schools and unregulated private school choice in creating "segregated" environments. So is "segregation" within schools that adopt apparently neutral policies that sort students based on different abilities and needs. Disparities in these contexts exist, and researchers tend not to dispute their existence. Yet, disparities continue despite laws that prohibit the inappropriate use of racial and other classifications.

The existence of permissible disparities reveals how legal doctrine reflects dominant societal beliefs. The legal system has difficulty addressing disparities because of its strong attachment to principles grounded in dominant societal beliefs. We already have seen the effects of the belief that the government should remain neutral in the manner it addresses group differences that it did not directly create. This belief has firm societal roots, as it derives from the belief that the government should leave people alone as much as possible. It rests on the concept of freedom and view that the government should not favor particular groups. Other influential and dominant beliefs also are important to consider. The commitment to opportunity and fair legal processes reveals how dominant societal beliefs guide the legal system and, in the end, contribute to group disparities.

Narrow Views of Opportunity

Like society, the legal system evinces a strong attachment to fair opportunities. However, regardless of how fair the individual components of the legal system can be, it cannot reach effectiveness if it plays down factors that influence differences in people's situations as they enter them. Nor can systems reach effectiveness if they ignore outcomes for the simple reason that opportunity may be inadequate if it predictably results in disparate outcomes. The strong belief in creating opportunities plays down a needed focus on outcomes as well as inputs.

The nature of the problems that arise when focusing on opportunities is well understood in policies addressing group disparities in schooling. Schools' tracking of children with special needs is illustrative. Identifying groups of children for special remediation can lead to groupings that run along ethnic and racial lines. As a result, schools aiming to address students' needs may foster differential treatment and segregated environments. This occurs because opportunity is narrowly defined in terms of opportunities given in school. An approach that would make a focus on opportunity more effective would also center on opportunities outside of schools (homes, communities, employment, nutrition, and safety) that would enhance opportunities once children begin school and maintain their performance when they progress through it. The point is that society and the legal system do embrace the need to ensure opportunity, which may be needed to address differential treatment, but the embrace is too narrow.

Narrow Visions of Responsibility

Another broad societal belief reflected in the legal system concerns the legitimacy of processes that determine the responsibility of individuals and institutions, including the government. The commitment to well-accepted processes is well known, as reflected in alleged criminal offenders' due process rights such as their right to counsel, fair trials, and other protections from erroneous deprivations of their basic rights. Remarkably, the criminally accused generally receive these protections even before the legal system would infringe on their rights. The legal system seeks to prevent unnecessary infringements. These due process protections play a key role in the justice system's ability to avoid inappropriate differential treatment based on race. In addition, they figure prominently in the civil contexts that seek to resolve disputes about rights violations, including inappropriate discrimination. Yet, concerns about due process may hamper the development of effective responses and counter efforts to ensure fair treatment.

In situations alleging inappropriate differential treatment, due process protections arise in efforts to assign responsibility. Generally, it means that the government wants to hold people responsible, but it works to ensure that it is holding the correct individuals responsible when assigning blame. This approach finds it unfair to stigmatize individuals or groups as "guilty" of discrimination unless it involves an element of moral blameworthiness. This need to assign individual blameworthiness renders courts reluctant to find discrimination, as it leads to raising very high barriers before establishing inappropriate discrimination. This perspective places more emphasis on the harm of being labeled a discriminator than on the harm caused by the discriminatory actions. Relatedly, the approach seeks to identify and catalog perpetrators to ensure proper ascription of the correct evils to the correct perpetrator. It focuses less on the victim's experience and their sense of unfair treatment and difficult circumstances. In many ways, when the legal system fails to ascribe responsibility to a specific "perpetrator" because they lack individual blameworthiness, responsibilities rest on the "victim" regardless of their actual blameworthiness for their circumstances. The legal system has created a default rule: It only holds those who are suffering victimization to blame and responsible for their circumstances; the rest are not to blame or avoid responsibility.

Two important corollaries attach to the focus on fair process and the search for the proper identification of villains who discriminate. The first corollary is that the focus on fault leads those not labeled perpetrators to believe in their innocence and disconnect from the problem. Not being categorized as a perpetrator leaves the categorization of innocent societal bystander. Narrowing on particular perpetrators makes it difficult to call more individuals to account or implicate in efforts to eradicate inequality. Again, without someone specifically identified as at fault, the ones who have been subjugated receive the blame. And that blame is what results in the second corollary. Viewing the subjugated as blameworthy diminishes the need for assisting; they are not even "victims." This process is not merely theoretical. It works at the foundation of legal responses and shapes their outcomes.

The narrow approach accounts for the current inability to address broad societal discrimination, as it is not viewed as discrimination at all. General societal discrimination is racial imbalance outside of the legal system's direct control. Approaching racial disparities as resulting from general societal discrimination also makes it difficult to enact race-conscious efforts, as seen in concerns raised by those who view these efforts as "reverse discrimination." In fact, these concerns are what led to the current focus on governmental neutrality rather than on affirmative stances that consider racial and ethnic characteristics.

The previous example of how due process works in instances of discrimination also reflects a narrow view of due process and the government's responsibility to ensure rights. A broader view of due process in the context of discrimination would involve a broader sense of what constitutes a deprivation of rights. When rights are deemed important enough, the legal system provides heightened protections, including resources to prevent erroneous deprivation of those rights. For example, the right to counsel and similar resources routinely expands into an affirmative obligation on the part of the government to support the right by providing needed resources to individuals unable to afford them. In terms of discrimination, it could include increasing access to minimal resources to assist in creating situations that would foster readiness for taking advantage of opportunities. We already know the sources of racial and ethnic disparities; a broader view of due process, on the government's affirmative obligations to protect rights, can help address them.

To be sure, arguments can be made against the government's incurring affirmative obligations; but such arguments need not go unchallenged. In the right to counsel context, the government essentially gains responsibility when individuals become suspects and the government is enlisting its resources that put individuals' rights at risk. The same approach finds parallels in other situations, such as the inability to hold the government responsible for private harms inflicted by individuals without direct links to the government (*DeShaney v. Winnebago*, 1989). However, this need not result in embracing a narrow approach to addressing racial disparities and only requiring remedies when the government directly caused them. There is no doubt, again, that racial disparities that occur in schooling occur during schooling regardless of their causes. Although the government may not be directly involved in matters that led to the different opportunities, it is difficult to ignore the government's role when it is directly involved in offering the education. The harm is the disparity in the education; the remedy is the reduction of that disparity. It is not entirely clear why current law, which requires direct government involvement, does not even find a harm worth remedying.

Resistance to Empirical Findings Reflects Unnecessary Acquiescence

The legal system, then, reflects societal assumptions and aspirations. That reflection accounts for the way that legal responses to social issues have developed and also for the responses to empirical research. The resistance to research occurs because of a preference to ignore it. That preference comports with broadly held claims that the legal system and basic rights are clearly denoted, founded on tradition, enduring, and resist change. But, again, that need not be the case. Rights are much more fluid than that, as exemplified by this very area of law that has been dramatically transformed from its initial conception. This conclusion may not sit well with those who prefer to focus mainly on legal rules and ignore empirical realities. However, the legal system undoubtedly can develop and make effective use of empirical findings.

The Legal System Can Better Fit Empirical Findings

Gaps between empirical findings and the legal system's approach to segregation are nothing short of bizarre. An empirical look at the legal system's effectiveness in addressing segregation reveals, from a practical perspective, that segregation persists and the legal system continues as though it does not. Even more bizarre, the negative effects of disparities are well documented, and the legal system compels itself to ignore much of them. In addition, the law does not square with people's experiences. People's experiences of discrimination do not match the law's definition of discrimination. Unlike the legal system, differentially treated individuals (including groups of individuals) do not necessarily care who treats them differently. They do not make distinctions between governmental actions and private actions, particularly not the close link the legal system needs between governmental actions and discrimination. Individuals who have been discriminated against do not find discrimination addressed if the recognition fails to improve their treatment. Recognizing the illegality of discrimination leads to the expectation of change, particularly relating to the conditions associated with past practices of discrimination. If conditions continue after the formal elimination of discrimination, then it is difficult to argue that it has been eliminated. The legal system appears to be operating in a different realm of reality from those who experience differential treatment.

Relevant Disputes Are Legal, Not Empirical

The bizarre gap between law and empirical findings does not seem attributable to disputes in empirical findings. Empirical research is not free from disputes. But the relevant disputes have to do with the legal system's approach, not the empirical findings themselves that reveal slices of reality. This is true regardless of whether the legal system adopts anti-classification or anti-subordination approaches. Several examples reveal how the legal disputes are at the core of issues, not the empirical findings.

The legal system adopts a narrow view of segregation, one that focuses on the legal system's direct classification of individuals into different groups based on race. The disputes relating to that approach are not empirical. Some studies show that sometimes being schooled in homogeneous groups can lead to more effective outcomes, including outcomes relating to mental health and achievement. Those findings are not in dispute. Similarly, disputes arise regarding the effectiveness of desegregation efforts. Numerous studies reveal that some forms of desegregation efforts have not led to the intended effects, as least for the youth involved. Those findings are not in dispute. What is in dispute is how the legal system desegregated and how it can make better use of findings that reveal how the legal system can more effectively achieve the benefits of desegregation.

Disputes also exist about the benefits of integration, of diversity itself. Sometimes integration leads to positive outcomes and sometimes to negative outcomes, depending on the specific outcomes of interest. The dispute is not about the findings but about which outcomes should be society's main concern. Regardless of those disputes, there is no doubt that differential treatment that oppresses one group is not beneficial to individuals in that group. Nor is there doubt that social responses that provide the same opportunities to everyone without accounting for initial differences contribute to differential outcomes. The dispute is about societal priorities.

Disputes also exist about the effectiveness of the legal system's neutral stances. These disputes have to do with the legal system's approach, not the empirical findings. For example, there is no doubt that stances that structure outcomes—such as controlled voucher systems—more likely lead to intended outcomes. Race-conscious efforts more likely effect race-conscious outcomes. The real dispute is whether the legal system will heed the lessons of research.

Law Can Embrace Undisputed Empirical Findings

Disputes relate to the way that the legal system has framed the evidence it needs, not the evidence itself. Legal approaches may reflect social acquiescence of particular ways of framing issues, but they need not be that way. Although reliance on research does bring its own challenges, it does provide alternative visions and approaches. If empirical research describes situations as problematic on racial status grounds, then it is unclear why the legal system can ignore them. A socially created system cannot be deemed effective if it ignores phenomena that ill-serve society and harms individuals. Even current legal rules, however, allow for the use of empirical research to shape legal decisions and policies relating to discrimination and racial disparities.

Legal standards remain considerably flexible. Much of the legal system is guided by myths of what it can and cannot do. The prevailing myth is that the legal system needs to be "color-blind" when it deals with people from different groups and with different needs. That just is not the case. The legal system need not treat different groups of people the same way in order to treat them equally. Basic legal parameters permit the use of empirical findings in at least three ways.

First, the strong attachment to neutrality can lead to support for apparently neutral policies that respond to empirically identified needs. This support encompasses the reach of a rather expansive and resource-rich government. It means that efforts to address disparities can be done through a very wide variety of ways that the legal system can use to influence how people treat each other. This means, for example, that socializing contexts can be enlisted to address disparities. That is what the legal system has done to address disparities in the juvenile justice system and child welfare system (Levesque, 2015). In the juvenile justice system, these efforts focus on supporting families, communities, and even peers to reduce inappropriate involvement in justice systems and the disparities that come from involvement in punitive governmental responses to circumstances linked to racial disparities (Levesque, 2014). In child welfare systems, much focus goes to helping preserve families through social and financial resources as well as through community, neighborhood, and religious groups (Levesque, 2008). All these efforts can be shaped in ways that address racial/ethnic disparities.

Second, other roles for empirical evidence can come through demonstrating the need for compelling interests to adopt narrowly tailored responses. Much empirical evidence reveals a need for race-conscious efforts. For example, in some circumstances, vouchers enhance the use of private biases and counter the reasons for using vouchers to foster diversity. In some contexts, vouchers will reach effectiveness only if they include elements of racial consciousness. Equally important, research can show the need for taking a broader view of opportunities as well as a broader approach to due process to protect from illegitimate infringements on people's rights. Notably, waiting until secondary school to address matters of diversity is too late.

Third, empirical research can help address private biases. Policies can be developed that help ensure individuals' recognition of inappropriate biases and actions. This comes from structuring decision-making so that individuals can consider how they make their decisions. Policies addressing discrimination already can do that. They can do more than simply prohibit discrimination; they can foster different social climates. School districts and private schools, for example, could take several important steps. Cultural competency training for teachers could ensure that they recognize the ways that their implicit biases may impact how they relate to and teach students from different backgrounds. Multicultural education practices could include the use of multicultural curriculum. Professional development for teachers and staff could include learning to build classroom communities in which students are respectful of each other's differences and learn from each other's diverse perspectives and experiences. Although these recommendations may be the typical ones offered by researchers (Levesque, 2015), the reality is that strategies that ignore these key components may produce integration on a surface level but will miss the true opportunity of integration. The government's interest in integration is to create learning environments rich with the diverse cultures, experiences, and strengths of students from different backgrounds. All students benefit from such environments. And, it just so happens that it is the type of school environment—the school climate—that accounts for many of the effects relating to the law's concerns for race relations, academic achievement, occupational attainment, and civic participation.

Conclusions

Two simple conclusions emerge from a look at empirical research and legal mandates relating to segregation in primary and secondary schools, including its related constructs such as racial imbalances, discrimination, and prejudice. The first conclusion is that legal responses have taken an air of inevitability and the second is that the legal system has difficulty facing empirical realities.

The conclusions are problematic for addressing the types of group disparities identified by researchers. The legal system embraces the conclusion that the government inevitably needs to remain neutral to disparities. Researchers challenge that conclusion. They reveal that, as it formally remains neutral in matters relating to race and ethnicity, the legal system spurs the use of private biases that individuals are free to hold and use, and it ignores different powers embedded in social situations. As a result, basic differences in experiences based on race have become more institutionalized, more covert, and seemingly based on characteristics that are nonracial. They have become normalized.

The fundamental dilemma that these twin conclusions raise is whether society wishes to remain committed to neutrality in its responses to racial and ethnic disparities and imbalances in educational opportunities. The commitment does allow for important freedoms and opportunities for youth. However, these different opportunities without doubt influence educational outcomes, which tend to be ignored as the legal system focuses on opportunity at the expense of results. The point is that efforts to remove the government from our lives leave disparities in opportunities, treatment, and outcomes. They ignore the government's already significant role in fostering these disparities and shaping important parts of people's realities.

The overall message emerging from an empirical look at school segregation and diversity laws challenges the fundamental legal lesson learned in this book. The fundamental lesson was that the legal system matters, that it frames issues and debates, and that it determines whether and when empirical evidence matters. However, that need not be the concluding message. The legal system merely reflects societal demands. This allows researchers to consider more closely the type of research needed to support societal goals. To do so, researchers must sort through legal rules to determine which are open to empirical analysis and accept that their work may lack relevance to legal disputes regardless of their scientific and social merit. Empirical findings that recognize their biases and consider legal needs can shape societal demands and offer ways to satisfy them. In this manner, and if they wish to do so, both research and the legal system can give full expression to the three words that begin and frame the US Constitution: *We the people.*

References

Chapter 1

Brown v. Board of Education (Brown I), 347 U.S. 483 (1954).
Brown v. Board of Education (Brown II), 349 U.S. 294 (1955).
Clotfelter, C. T. (2001). Are Whites still fleeing? Racial patterns and enrollment shifts in urban public schools, 1987–1996. *Journal of Policy Analysis & Management, 20*, 199–221.
Clotfelter, C. T. (2004). *After Brown: The rise and retreat of school desegregation*. Princeton, NJ: Princeton University Press.
Frankenberg, E., Lee, C., & Orfield, G. (2003). *A multiracial society with segregated schools: Are we losing the dream*. Cambridge, MA: Civil Rights Project, Harvard University.
Kim, C. Y., Losen, D. J., & Hewitt, D. T. (2010). *The school-to-prison pipeline: Structuring legal reform*. New York, NY: New York University Press.
Levesque, R. J. R. (2014). Discrimination, developmental science, and the law: Addressing dramatic shifts in civil rights jurisprudence. *American Journal of Orthopsychiatry, 84*, 25–34.
Levesque, R. J. R. (2015). *Adolescence, discrimination, and the law: Addressing dramatic shifts in equality jurisprudence*. New York, NY: New York University Press.
Lutz, B. F. (2011). The end of court-ordered desegregation. *American Economic Journal: Economic Policy, 3*, 130–168.
Minow, M. (2010). *In Brown's wake: Legacies of America's educational landmark*. New York, NY: Oxford University Press.
Moran, R. F. (2010). What Counts As Knowledge? A Reflection on Race, Social Science, and the Law. *Law & Society Review, 44*, 515–552.

Orfield, G., & Frankenberg, E. (2014). Increasingly segregated and unequal schools as courts reverse policy. *Educational Administration Quarterly, 50*, 718–734.
Parents Involved in Community Schools v. Seattle School District No. 1, 551 U.S. 701 (2007).
Plessy v. Ferguson, 163 U.S. 537 (1896).
Reardon, S. F., Grwal, E. T., Kalogrides, D., & Greenberg, E. (2012). Brown fades: The end of court-ordered school desegregation and the resegregation of American public schools. *Journal of Policy Analysis and Management, 31*, 876–904.
Reardon, S. F., & Owens, A. (2014). 60 Years after *Brown*: Trends and consequences of school segregation. *Annual Review of Sociology, 40*, 199–218.
Stroub, K. J., & Richards, M. P. (2013). From resegregation to reintegration: Trends in the racial/ethnic segregation of metropolitan public schools, 1993–2009. *American Educational Research Journal, 50*, 497–531.
Walsemann, K. M., & Bell, B. A. (2010). Integrated schools, segregated curriculum: Effects of within-school segregation on adolescent health behaviors and educational aspirations. *American Journal of Public Health, 100*, 1687–1695.

Chapter 2

Adarand Constructors, Inc. v. Peña, 515 U.S. 200 (1995).
Bolling v. Sharpe, 347 U.S. 497 (1954).
Bowers v. Hardwick, 478 U.S. 186 (1986).
Brown v. Board of Education (Brown I), 347 U.S. 483 (1954).
City of Richmond v. J. A. Croson Co., 488 U.S. 469 (1989).
Cleburne v. Cleburne Living Center, Inc., 473 U.S. 432 (1985).
Craig v. Boren, 429 U.S. 190 (1976).
Employment Division v. Smith, 494 U.S. 872 (1990).
FCC v. Beach Communications, Inc., 508 U.S. 307 (1993).
Fisher v. University of Texas at Austin (Fisher II), No. 14–981 (2016).
Graham v. Richardson, 403 U.S. 365 (1971).
Gratz v. Bollinger, 539 U.S. 244 (2003).
Green v. County School Board of New Kent County, 391 U.S. 430 (1968).
Grutter v. Bollinger, 539 U.S. 306 (2003).
Gunther, G. (1972). The Supreme Court, 1971 term—Foreword: In search of evolving doctrine on a changing court: A model for a newer equal protection. *Harvard Law Review, 86*, 1–48, 50–306.
J.E.B. v. Alabama, 511 U.S. 127 (1994).
Korematsu v. United States, 323 U.S. 214 (1944).
Lawrence v. Texas, 539 US 558 (2003).
Mississippi University for Women v. Hogan, 458 U.S. 718 (1982).
New York State Board of Elections v. Lopez Torres, 552 U.S. 196 (2008).
Obergefell v. Hodges, Supreme Court No. 14–556 (June 26, 2015).
Parents Involved in Community Schools v. Seattle School District No. 1, 551 U.S. 701 (2007).

Plyler v. Doe, 457 U.S. 202 (1982).
Reed v. Campbell, 476 U.S. 852 (1986).
Regents of the University of California v. Bakke, 438 U. S. 265 (1978).
Romer v. Evans, 517 U.S. 620 (1996).
San Antonio Independent School District v. Rodriguez, 411 U.S. 1 (1973).
Slaughter-House Cases, 83 U.S. (16 Wall.) 36 (1873).
Strauder v. West Virginia, 100 U.S. 303 (1880).
Sweatt v. Painter, 339 U.S. 629 (1950).
United States v. Carolene Products Company, 304 U.S. 144 (1938).
United States v. Virginia, 518 U.S. 515 (1996).

Chapter 3

Brown v. Board of Education (Brown I), 347 U.S. 483 (1954).
Brown v. Board of Education (Brown II), 349 U.S. 294 (1955).
Fisher v. the University of Texas at Austin (Fisher II), No. 14–981 (2016).
Gratz v. Bollinger, 539 U.S. 244 (2003).
Grutter v. Bollinger, 539 U.S. 306 (2003).
Halpern, D. F., Eliot, L., Bigler, R. S., Fabes, R. A., Hanish, L. D., Hyde, J., . . . Martin, C. L. (2011). The pseudoscience of single-sex schooling. *Science, 333*, 1706–1707.
Kiang, L., Witkow, M. R., Baldelomar, O. A., & Fuligni, A. J. (2010). Change in ethnic identity across the high school years among adolescents with Latin American, Asian, and European backgrounds. *Journal of Youth and Adolescence, 39*, 683–693.
Logan, J. R., Oakley, D., & Stowell, J. (2008). School segregation in metropolitan regions, 1970–2000: The impacts of policy choices on public education. *American Journal of Sociology, 113*, 1611–1644.
Mickelson, R. (2003). When are racial disparities in education the result of racial discrimination? A social science perspective. *Teachers College Record, 105*, 1052–1086.
Parents Involved in Community Schools v. Seattle School District No. 1, 551 U.S. 701 (2007).
Reardon, S. F., & Owens, A. (2014). 60 years after Brown: Trends and consequences of school segregation. *Annual Review of Sociology, 40*, 199–218.
Regents of the University of California v. Bakke, 438 U.S. 265 (1978).

Chapter 4

Agirdag, O., Demanet, J., Van Houtte, M., & Van Avermaet, P. (2011). Ethnic school composition and peer victimization: A focus on the interethnic school climate. *International Journal of Intercultural Relations, 35*, 465–473.
Alexander, K., & Schofield, J. W. (2006). Stereotype threat: How students' responses to perceived negative stereotypes undermine their achievement. In J. W. Schofield (Ed.), *Migration background, minority-group membership and academic achievement: Research evidence from social, educational, and*

developmental psychology (pp. 13–42). Berlin, Germany: Social Science Research Center Berlin.

Allport, G. W. (1954). *The nature of prejudice*. Garden City, NJ: Doubleday.

Antonio, A. L., Chang, M. J., Hakuta, K., Kenny, D. A., Levin, S., & Milem, J. F. (2004). Effects of racial diversity on complex thinking in college students. *Psychological Science, 15*, 507–510.

Armor, D. J. (1984). The evidence on desegregation and Black achievement. In T. Cook et al. (Eds.), *School desegregation and Black achievement* (pp. 43–67). Washington, DC: National Institution of Education.

Armor, D. J. (2006). Lessons learned from school desegregation. In P. Peterson (Ed.), *Generational change: Closing the test score gap* (pp. 115–142). Lanham, MD: Rowman & Littlefield.

Bachman, J. G., O'Malley, P. M., Freedman-Doan, P., Trzesniewski, K. H., & Donnellan, M. B. (2011). Adolescent self-esteem: Differences by race/ethnicity, gender, and age. *Self and Identity, 10*(4), 445–473.

Benner, A., & Crosnoe, R. (2011). The racial/ethnic composition of elementary schools and young children's academic and socioemotional functioning. *American Educational Research Journal, 48*(3), 621–646.

Berends, M., & Penaloza, R. V. (2010). Increasing racial isolation and test score gaps in mathematics: A 30-year perspective. *Teachers College Record, 112*, 979–1007.

Black, C. (1960). The lawfulness of the segregation decisions. *Yale Law Journal, 69*, 421–430.

Borman, G., & Dowling, M. (2010). Schools and inequality: A multilevel analysis of Coleman's equality of educational opportunity data. *Teachers College Record, 112*, 1201–1246.

Borman, K. M., McNulty-Eitle, T., Michael, D., Eitle, D. J., Lee, R., Johnson, L., . . . Shircliffe, B. (2004). Accountability in a postdesegregation era: The continuing significance of racial segregation in Florida's schools. *American Educational Research Journal, 41*, 605–631.

Bowman, N. A. (2010). College diversity experiences and cognitive development: A meta-analysis. *Review of Educational Research, 80*, 4–33.

Bowman, N. A. (2011). Promoting participation in a diverse democracy: A meta-analysis of college diversity experiences and civic engagement. *Review of Educational Research, 81*, 29–68.

Bowman, N. A., & Denson, N. (2012). What's past is prologue: How precollege exposure to diversity shapes the impact of college diversity experiences. *Research in Higher Education, 53*, 406–425.

Braddock, J. H., III, & Eitle, T. M. (2004). The effects of school desegregation. In J. Banks & C. A. McGee Banks (Eds.), *Handbook of research on multicultural education* (pp. 828–843). San Francisco, CA: Jossey-Bass.

Braddock, J.H., III, & Gonzales, A. D. C. (2010). Social isolation and social cohesion: The effects of K–12 neighborhood and school segregation on intergroup orientations. *Teachers College Record, 112*, 1631–1653.

Braddock, J. H., III, & McPartland, J. (1989). Social psychological processes that perpetuate racial segregation. *Journal of Black Studies, 19*, 267–289.

Bradley, L. A., & Bradley, G. W. (1977). The academic achievement of Black students in desegregated schools: A critical review. *Review of Educational Research, 47*, 399–451.

Brown v. Board of Education, 347 U.S. 483 (1954).
Buck, S. (2010). *Acting White: The ironic legacy of desegregation*. New Haven, CT: Yale University Press.
Byrd, C. M., & Tabbye, C. (2011). Racial identity, school racial climate, and school intrinsic motivation among African American youth: The importance of person–context congruence. *Journal of Research on Adolescence, 21*, 849–860.
Caldas, J. S., & Bankston, C. (1998). The inequality of separation: Racial composition of schools and academic achievement. *Educational Administration Quarterly, 34*, 533–557.
Campbell, D. (2005). Vote early, vote often: The role of schools in creating civic norms. *Education Next, 5*, 62–69.
Campbell, D. (2006). *Why we vote: How schools and communities shape our civic life*. Princeton, NJ: Princeton University Press.
Campbell, D. (2007). Sticking together: Classroom diversity and civic education. *American Politics Research, 35*, 57–78.
Campbell, D. (2009). An empirical test of the sorting model. *American Political Science Review, 53*, 771–786.
Carter, R. L. (1953). The effects of segregation and the consequences of desegregation: A social science statement. *Journal of Negro Education, 22*, 68–76.
Choi, K., Raley, K., Muller, C., & Riegle-Crumb, C. (2008). Class composition: Socioeconomic characteristics of coursemates and college enrollment. *Social Science Quarterly, 89*, 846–866.
Clark, K. B., Chein, I., & Cook, S. W. (1952). The effects of segregation and the consequences of desegregation A (September 1952) social science statement in the *Brown v. Board of Education of Topeka* Supreme Court case. *American Psychologist, 59*, 495–501.
Cohen, E. G. (1975). The effects of desegregation on race relations. *Law and Contemporary Problems, 39*, 271–299.
Coleman, J., Campbell, E. Q., Hobson, C., McPartland, J., Mood, A., Winfield, F., & York, R. (1966). *Equality of educational opportunity*. Washington, DC: US Government Printing Office.
Cook, T. (1984). *School desegregation and Black achievement*. Washington, DC: US Department of Education.
Crain, R. L., & Mahard, R. (1978). Desegregation and Black achievement: A review of the research. *Law and Contemporary Problems, 42*, 17–55.
Crain, R. L., & Mahard, R. (1983). The effect of research methodology on desegregation achievement studies: A meta-analysis. *American Journal of Sociology, 88*, 839–854.
Darling-Hammond, L. (2010). *The flat world and education: How America's commitment to equity will determine our future*. New York, NY: Teachers College Press.
Deutscher, M., & Chein, I. (1948). The psychological effects of enforced segregation: A survey of social science opinion. *Journal of Psychology, 26*, 259–287.
Ehrmann, N., & Massey, D. (2008). Gender-specific effects of ecological conditions on college achievement. *Social Science Research, 37*, 220–238.

Eitle, D., & Eitle, T. M. (2003). Segregation and school violence. *Social Forces, 82*, 589–615.
Epps, E. G. (1975). Impact of school desegregation on aspirations, self-concepts, and other aspects of personality. *Law and Contemporary Problems, 39*, 300–313.
Epps, E. G. (1978). The impact of school desegregation on the self-evaluation and achievement orientation of minority children. *Law and Contemporary Problems, 42*, 57–76.
Epps, E. G. (1981). Minority children: Desegregation, self-evaluation, and achievement orientation. In W. Hawley (Ed.), *Effective school desegregation* (pp. 85–106). Beverly Hills, CA: Sage.
Feld, S., & Carter, W. (1998). When desegregation reduces interracial contact. *American Journal of Sociology, 103*, 1165–1186.
Fordham, S., & Ogbu, J. (1986). Black students' school success: Coping with the burden of acting White. *Urban Review, 18*, 176–206.
Frost, M. B. (2007). Texas students' college expectations: Does high school composition matter? *Sociology of Education, 80*, 43–65.
Fryer, R. G., & Torelli, P. (2006). *An empirical analysis of "acting White."* NBER Working Paper 11334. Cambridge, MA: National Bureau of Economic Research.
Gerard, H., & Miller, N. (1975). *School desegregation: A long-term study.* New York, NY: Plenum.
Goldsmith, P. A. (2003). All segregation is not equal: The impact of Latino and Black school composition. *Sociological Perspectives, 46*, 83–105.
Goldsmith, P. A. (2004). Schools' role in shaping race relations: Evidence of friendliness and conflict. *Social Problems, 51*, 587–612.
Goldsmith, P. R. (2010). Learning apart, living apart: The lasting impact of perpetual segregation. *Teachers College Record, 112*, 1602–1630.
Graham, S. (2006). Peer victimization in school: Exploring the ethnic context. *Current Directions in Psychological Science, 15*, 317–321.
Gray-Little, B., & Hafdahl, A. R. (2000). Factors influencing racial comparisons of self-esteem: A quantitative review. *Psychological Bulletin, 126*(1), 26–54.
Gregor, A. J. (1963). The law, social science, and school segregation: An assessment. *Western Reserve Law Review, 14*, 635–636.
Gurin, P., Dey, E. L., Hurtado, S., & Gurin, G. (2002). Diversity and higher education: Theory and impact in educational outcomes. *Harvard Educational Review, 72*, 330–367.
Gurin, P., Nagda, B., & Lopez, G. (2004). The benefits of diverse education for democratic citizenship. *Journal of Social Issues, 60*, 17–34.
Guryan, J. (2004). Desegregation and Black dropout rates. *American Economic Review, 94*, 919–943.
Gutmann, A. (1999). *Democratic education.* Princeton. NJ: Princeton University Press.
Hanish, L. D., & Guerra, N. G. (2000). The roles of ethnicity and school context in predicting children's victimization by peers. *American Journal of Community Psychology, 28*, 201–223.
Hanushek, E. A., Kain, J. F., & Rivkin, S. G. (2009). New evidence about *Brown v. Board of Education*: The complex effects of school racial composition on achievement. *Journal of Labor Economics, 27*, 349–383.

Holmes, J. J., Wells, A. S., & Revilla, A. T. (2005). Learning through experience: What graduates gained by attending desegregated high schools. i14–24.

Horn, C., & Kurlaender, M. (2006). *The end of Keyes—Resegregation trends and achievement in Denver public schools*. Cambridge, MA: The Civil Rights Project.

Hurtado, S. (2005). The next generation of diversity and intergroup relations research. *Journal of Social Issues*, *61*, 595–610.

Hurtado, S., Engberg, M., Ponjuan, L., & Landreman, L. (2002). Students' precollege preparation for participation in a diverse democracy. *Research in Higher Education*, *43*, 163–186.

Jackson, K. (2009). Student demographics, teacher sorting, and teacher quality: Evidence from the end of desegregation. *Journal of Labor Economics*, *27*, 313–328.

Junn, J. (2004). Diversity, immigration, and the politics of civic education. *PS: Political Science & Politics*, *37*, 253–255.

Kahne, J., Chi, B., & Middaugh, E. (2006). Building social capital for civic and political engagement: The potential of high school civics courses. *Canadian Journal of Education*, *29*, 387–409.

Kurlaender, M., & Yun, J. (2001). Is diversity a compelling educational interest? Evidence from Louisville. In G. Orfield (Ed.), *Diversity challenged: Evidence on the impact of affirmative action* (pp. 111–141). Cambridge, MA: Harvard Education.

Kurlaender, M., & Yun, J. (2005). Fifty years after *Brown*: New evidence of the impact of school racial composition on student outcomes. *International Journal of Educational Policy, Research and Practice*, *6*, 51–78.

Kurlaender, M., & Yun, J. (2007). Measuring school racial composition and student outcomes in a multiracial society. *American Journal of Education*, *113*, 213–242.

Ladwig, J. G. (2010). Beyond academic outcomes. *Review of Research in Education*, *34*, 113–141.

LaFree, G., & Arum, R. (2006). The impact of racially inclusive schooling on adult incarceration rates among U.S. cohorts of African Americans and Whites since 1930. *Criminology*, *44*, 73–103.

Levesque, R. J. R. (2002). Dangerous adolescents, model adolescents: Shaping the role and promise of education. New York, NY: Plenum/Kluwer.

Linn, R. L., & Welner, K. G. (Eds.). (2007). *Race-conscious policies for assigning students to schools: Social science research and the Supreme Court cases*. Washington, DC: National Academy of Education.

Longshore, D., & Prager, J. (1985). The impact of school desegregation: A situational analysis. *Annual Review of Sociology*, *11*, 75–91.

Lotan, R. A. (2004). Stepping into groupwork. In E. G. Cohen, C. Brody, & M. Sapon-Shevin (Eds.), *Teaching cooperative learning: The challenge for teacher education* (pp. 167–182). Albany, NY: State University of New York Press.

Martin, I., Karabel, J., & Jaquez, S. W. (2005). High school segregation and access to the University of California. *Educational Policy*, *19*, 308–330.

Massey, D. (2006). Social background and academic and performance differentials: White and minority students at selective colleges. *Ethnic and Racial Studies*, *29*, 1–26.

Massey, D., & Fischer, M. (2006). The effect of childhood segregation on minority academic performance at selective colleges. *American Law and Economics Review, 8*, 390–409.
Mayer, S. (1991). How much does a high school's racial and socioeconomic mix affect graduation and teenage fertility? In C. Jencks & P. Peterson (Eds.), *The urban underclass* (pp. 321–341). Washington, DC: Brookings Institution Press.
McConahay, J. B. (1978). The effects of school desegregation upon student racial attitudes and behavior: A critical review of the literature and a prolegomenon to future research. *Law and Contemporary Problems, 42*, 77–107.
McNeil, L. (1986). *Contradictions of control: School structure and school knowledge*. New York, NY: Routledge & Kegan Paul.
Mickelson, R. A. (2008). Twenty-first century social science research on school diversity and educational outcomes. *Ohio State Law Journal, 69*, 1173–1228.
Mickelson, R. A. (2001). Subverting *Swann*: First- and second-generation segregation in Charlotte, North Carolina. *American Educational Research Journal, 38*, 215–252.
Mickelson, R. A., & Bottia, M. (2010). Integrated education and mathematics outcomes: A synthesis of social science research. *North Carolina Law Review, 87*, 993–1089.
Mickelson, R. A., Bottia, M. C., & Lambert, R. (2013). Effects of school racial composition on K–12 mathematics outcomes: A metaregression analysis. *Review of Educational Research, 83*, 121–158.
Mickelson, R. A., & Nkomo, M. (2012). Integrated schooling, life course outcomes, and social cohesion in multiethnic democratic societies. *Review of Research in Education, 36*, 1197–1238.
Miller, N., & Carlson, M. (1984). School desegregation as a social reform: A meta-analysis of its effects on Black academic achievement. In T. Cook, et al. (Eds.), *School desegregation and Black achievement* (pp. 89–130). Washington, DC: National Institute of Education.
Newton, X. (2010). End-of-high-school mathematics attainment: How did students get there? *Teachers College Record, 112*, 1064–1095.
Oates, G. (2004). The color of the undergraduate experience and the Black self-concept: Evidence from longitudinal data. *Social Psychology Quarterly, 67*, 16–32.
Oliver, E. (2010). *Paradoxes of integration: Race, neighborhood and civic life in multiethnic America*. Chicago, IL: University of Chicago Press.
Orfield, G., & Lee, C. (2004). *Brown at 50: King's dream or Plessy's nightmare?* Cambridge, MA: Harvard Civil Rights Project.
Parents Involved in Community Schools v. Seattle School District No. 1, 551 U.S. 701 (2007).
Pascarella, E. T., Salisbury, M. H., Martin, G. L., & Blaich, C. (2012). Some complexities in the effects of diversity experiences on orientation toward social/political activism and political views in the first year of college. *Journal of Higher Education, 83*(4), 467–496.
Pettigrew, T. F., & Tropp, L. R. (2006). A meta-analytic test of intergroup contact theory. *Journal of Personality and Social Psychology, 90*, 751–783.

Pettigrew, T. F., & Tropp, L. R. (2008). How does intergroup contact reduce prejudice? Meta-analytic tests of three mediators. *European Journal of Social Psychology, 38*, 922–934.

Proahansky, H., & Newton, P. (1968). The nature and meaning of Negro self-identity. In M. Deutsch, I. Katz, & A. R. Jensen (Eds.), *Social class, race and psychological development* (pp. 178–218). New York, NY: Holt, Rinehart & Winston.

Quillian, L., & Campbell, M. E. (2003). Beyond Black and White: The present and future of multiracial friendship segregation. *American Sociological Review, 68*, 540–566.

Reardon, S. F., & Owens, A. (2014). 60 years after *Brown*: Trends and consequences of school segregation. *Annual Review of Sociology, 40*, 199–218.

Regents of the University of California v. Bakke, 438 U.S. 265 (1978).

Reyes, M. R., Brackett, M. A., Rivers, S. E., White, M., & Salovey, P. (2012). Classroom emotional climate, student engagement, and academic achievement. *Journal of Educational Psychology, 104*, 700–712.

Rosenberg, M., & Simmons, R. G. (1972). *Black and White self-esteem: The urban school child.* Washington, DC: American Sociological Association.

Rossell, C., Armor, D., & Walberg, H. (2001). *Twenty-first century desegregation.* New York, NY: Oxford University Press.

Rumberger, R., & Palardy, G. (2005). Does segregation still matter? The impact of student composition on academic achievement in high school. *Teachers College Record, 107*, 1999–2045.

Ryan, A. M. (2000). Peer groups as a context for the socialization of adolescents' motivation, engagement and achievement in school. *Educational Psychologist, 35*, 101–111.

Saatcioglu, A. (2010). The hidden value of school desegregation: Disentangling school-and student-level effects of desegregation and resegregation on the dropout problem in urban high schools: Evidence from the Cleveland Municipal School District, 1977–1998. *Teachers College Record, 112*, 1391–1442.

Schofield, J. W. (1978). School desegregation and intergroup attitudes. In D. Bar-Tal & L. Saxe (Eds.), *Social psychology of education: Theory and research* (pp. 330–363). Washington, DC: Halsted Press.

Schofield, J. W. (1995). Review of research on school desegregation's impact on elementary and secondary school students. In J. A. Banks & C. A. M. Banks (Eds.), *Handbook of research on multicultural education* (pp. 597–616). New York, NY: Macmillan.

Schofield, J. W. (2001). Maximizing the benefits of a diverse student body: Lessons from school desegregation research. In G. Orfield (Ed.), *Diversity challenged* (pp. 99–110). Cambridge, MA: Harvard Education Publishing Group.

Schofield, J. W., & Eurich-Fulcer, R. (2002). When and how school desegregation improves intergroup relations. In R. Brown & S. Gaertner (Eds.), *Blackwell handbook of social psychology: Intergroup processes* (pp. 475–494). Malden, MA: Blackwell.

Shin, R., Daly, B., & Vera, E. (2007). The relationships of peer norms, ethnic identity, and peer support to school engagement in urban youth. *Professional School Counseling, 10*, 379–388.

St. John, N. (1975). *School desegregation: Outcomes for children*. New York, NY: Wiley.

Stearns, E. (2010). Long-term correlates of high school racial composition: Perpetuation theory reexamined. *Teachers College Record, 112*, 1654–1678.

Stearns, E., Buchmann, C., & Bonneau, K. (2009). Interracial friendships in the transition to college: Do birds of a feather flock together? *Sociology of Education, 82*, 173–195.

Steele, C., & Aronson, J. (1995). Stereotype threat and the intellectual performance of African-Americans. *Journal of Personality and Social Psychology, 69*, 797–811.

Stephan, W. G. (1978). School desegregation: An evaluation of predictions made in *Brown v. Board of Education*. *Psychological Bulletin, 85*, 217–238.

Tam, M. Y. S., & Bassett, G. W. (2004). Does diversity matter? Measuring the impact of high school diversity on freshman GPA. *Policy Studies Journal, 32*, 129–143.

Teranishi, R. T., & Parker, T. L. (2010). Social reproduction of inequality: Racial segregation, secondary schools, and postsecondary opportunities. *Teachers College Record, 112*, 1575–1601.

Terenzini, P., Cabrera, A., Colbeck, C., Bjorklund, S., & Parenti, J. (2001). Racial diversity in the classroom: Does it promote student learning? *Journal of Higher Education, 72*, 509–531.

Tinker v. Des Moines Independent Community School District, 393 U.S. 503 (1969).

Tropp, L. R., & Prenovost, M. A. (2008). The role of intergroup contact in predicting children's interethnic attitudes: Evidence from meta-analytic and field studies. In S. R. Levy & M. Killen (Eds.), *Intergroup attitudes and relations in childhood through adulthood* (pp. 236–248). New York, NY: Oxford University Press.

Ueno, K. (2009). Same-race friendships and school attachment: Demonstrating the interaction between personal network and school composition. *Sociological Forum, 24*, 515–537.

van den Haag, E. (1960). Social science testimony in the desegregation cases—A reply to Professor Kenneth Clark. *Villanova Law Review, 6*, 69–79.

Vervoort, M. H. M., Scholte, R. H. J., & Overbeek, G. (2010). Bullying and victimization among adolescents: The role of ethnicity and ethnic composition of school class. *Journal of Youth and Adolescence, 39*, 1–11.

Vigdor, J. L., & Ludwig, J. (2008). Segregation and the test score gap. In K. Magnuson & J. Waldfogel (Eds.), *Steady gains and stalled progress: Inequality and the Black–White test score gap* (pp. 181–211). New York, NY: Russell Sage Foundation.

Wechsler, H. (1959). Toward neutral principles of constitutional law. *Harvard Law Review, 73*, 1–35.

Weinberg, M. (1975). The relationship between school desegregation and academic achievement: A review of the research. *Law and Contemporary Problems, 39*, 240–270.

Weinberg, M. (1977). *Minority students: A research appraisal*. Washington, DC: National Institute of Education, Department of Health, Education and Welfare.

Wells, A. S., Holmes, J. J., Revilla, A. T., & Atanda, K. (2009). *Both sides now: The story of school desegregation graduates*. Berkeley, CA: University of California Press.
Wells, R. (2010). Children of immigrants and educational expectations: The role of school composition. *Teachers College Record, 112*, 1679–1704.
Welner, K. G. (2006). K–12 race-conscious student assignment policies: Law, social science and diversity. *Review of Research in Education, 76*, 349–382.
Welner, K. G. (2001). *Legal rights, local wrongs: When community control collides with educational equity*. Albany, NY: State University of New York Press.
Wentzel, K. R. (1989). Adolescent classroom goals, standards for performance and academic achievement: An interactionist perspective. *Journal of Educational Psychology, 81*, 131–142.
Wigfield, A., & Eccles, J. S. (2002). Students' motivation during the middle school years. In J. Aronson (Ed.), *Improving academic achievement: Impact of psychological factors on education* (pp. 160–185). San Diego, CA: Academic Press.
Wortman, P. M. (1984). School desegregation and Black achievement: An integrative view. In T. Cook et al. (Eds.), *School desegregation and Black achievement* (pp. 194–224). Washington, DC: National Institute of Education.
Yun, J., & Moreno, J. F. (2006). College access, K–12 concentrated disadvantage, and the next 25 years of education research. *Educational Researcher, 35*, 12–19.
Zirkel, P. A. (1971). Self concept and the "disadvantage" of ethnic group membership and mixture. *Review of Educational Research, 41*, 211–225.

Chapter 5

Allport, G. W. (1954). *The nature of prejudice*. Garden City, NJ: Doubleday.
Armor, D. J. (1980). White flight and the future of school desegregation. In W. Stephan & J. Fagin (Eds.), *School desegregation: Past, present and future* (pp. 187–226). New York, NY: Springer.
Ayscue, J. B., & Orfield, G. (2015). School district lines stratify educational opportunity by race and poverty. *Race and Social Problems, 7*, 5–20.
Brown, K. D. (2014). *Because of Our Success: The Changing Racial and Ethnic Ancestry of Blacks on Affirmative Action*. Durham, NC: Carolina Academic Press.
Christenson, B., et al. (2003). *Evaluation of the Magnet Schools Assistance Program, 1998 grantees*. Washington, DC: US Department of Education. Retrieved August 4, 2015, from https://www2.ed.gov/rschstat/eval/choice/magneteval/finalreport.pdf
Clotfelter, C. T. (1976). School desegregation, "tipping," and private school enrollment. *Journal of Human Resources, 11*, 28–50.
Cobb, C. D., & Glass, G. V. (2009). School choice in a post-desegregation world. *Peabody Journal of Education, 84*, 262–279.
Coleman, J. S. (1975). *Trends in school segregation, 1968–1973*. Washington, DC: Urban Institute.

Crosnoe, R. (2009). Low-income students and the socioeconomic composition of public high schools. *American Sociological Review, 74*, 709–730.
Davis, L. E., Strube, M. J., & Cheng, L. C. (1995). Too many Blacks, too many Whites: Is there a racial balance? *Basic and Applied Social Psychology, 17*, 119–135.
Duncan, G. J., & Magnuson, K. A. (2005). Can family socioeconomic resources account for racial and ethnic test score gaps? *Future of Children, 15*, 35–53.
Farley, R., Schuman, H., Bianchi, S., Colasanto, D., & Hatchett, S. (1978). "Chocolate city, vanilla suburbs": Will the trend toward racially separate communities continue? *Social Science Research, 7*, 319–344.
Fisher v. the University of Texas at Austin (Fisher I), 133 S.Ct. 2411 (2013).
Fisher v. the University of Texas at Austin (Fisher II), No. 14–981 (2016).
Frankenberg, E., & Lee, C. (2003, September). Charter schools and race: A lost opportunity for integrated education. *Education Policy Analysis Archives, 11*(32). Retrieved from http://epaa.asu.edu/ojs/article/viewFile/260/386; accessed July 7, 2013.
Glazerman, S. (1997). *A conditional logit model of elementary school choice: What do parents value?* Chicago, IL: University of Chicago, Harris School of Public Policy.
Gratz v. Bollinger, 539 U.S. 244 (2003).
Grutter v. Bollinger, 539 U.S. 306 (2003).
Hanish, L. D., & Guerra, N. G. (2000). The roles of ethnicity and school context in predicting children's victimization by peers. *American Journal of Community Psychology, 28*, 201–223.
Henig, J. (1990). Choice in public schools: An analysis of transfer requests among magnet schools. *Social Science Quarterly, 71*, 69–82.
Henig, J. (1996). The local dynamics of choice: Ethnic preferences and institutional responses. In B. Fuller, R. Elmore, & G. Orfield (Eds.), *Who chooses? Who loses? Culture, institutions, and the unequal effects of school choice* (pp. 95–117). New York, NY: Teachers College Press.
Hochschild, J., & Scovronick, D. (2003). *The American dream and the public schools*. New York, NY: Oxford University Press.
Hopwood v. Texas, 78 F.3d 932 (5th Cir. 1996).
Horn, J., & Miron, G. (2000). *An evaluation of Michigan's charter school initiative: Performance, accountability, and impact*. Kalamazoo, MI: Western Michigan University, Evaluation Center.
Howe, K., Eisenhart, M., & Betebenner, D. (2001). School choice crucible: A case study of Boulder Valley. *Phi Delta Kappan, 83*, 137–146.
Koedel, C., Betts, J. R., Rice, L. A., & Zau, A. C. (2009). The integrating and segregating effects of school choice. *Peabody Journal of Education, 84*, 110–129.
Lee, V., & Burkham, D. (2002). *Inequality at the starting gate: Social background differences in achievement as children begin school*. Washington, DC: Economic Policy Institute.
Levesque, J. R. (2015). *Adolescence, discrimination, and the law: Addressing dramatic shifts in equality jurisprudence*. New York, NY: New York University Press.
Li, M. (2009). Is there "white flight" into private schools? New evidence from high school and beyond. *Economics of Education Review, 28*, 382–392.

Linn, R. L., & Welner, K. G. (Eds.). (2007). *Race-conscious policies for assigning students to schools: Social science research and the Supreme Court cases.* Washington, DC: National Academy of Education.

McConahay, J. (1981). Reducing prejudice in desegregated schools. In W. Hawley (Ed.), *Effective school desegregation: Equity, quality and feasibility* (pp. 35–53). Beverly Hills, CA: Sage.

Miller v. Johnson, 515 U.S. 900 (1995).

Ni, H. (2012). The sorting effect of charter schools on student composition in traditional public schools. *Educational Policy, 26*, 215–242.

No Child Left Behind Act of 2001, Title V, Part C, 115 Stat. 1806, 20 U. S. C. §7231 et seq. (2000 ed., Supp. IV); 34 CFR §§280.2, 280.4 (2006).

Parents Involved in Community Schools v. Seattle School District No. 1, 551 U.S. 701 (2007).

Pettigrew, T., & Green, R. L. (1976). School desegregation in large cities: A critique of the Coleman "White flight" thesis. *Harvard Educational Review, 46*, 1–53.

Powell, J. A., & Menendian, S. (2014). *Fisher v. Texas*: The limits of exhaustion and the future of race-conscious university admissions. *University of Michigan Journal of Law Reform, 47*, 899.

Reardon, S. F., Yun, J. T., & Kurleander, M. (2006). Implications of income-based school assignment policies for racial school segregation. *Education Evaluation and Policy Analysis, 28*, 49–75.

Regents of the University of California v. Bakke, 438 U.S. 265 (1978).

Richards, M. P. (2014). The gerrymandering of school attendance zones and the segregation of public schools: A Geospatial Analysis. *American Educational Research Journal, 51*, 1119–1157.

Rivkin, S. (1994). Residential segregation and school integration. *Sociology of Education, 67*, 279–292.

Saporito, S. (2003). Private choices, public consequences: Magnet school choice and segregation by race and poverty. *Social Problems, 50*, 181–203.

Saporito, S., & Lareau, A. (1999). School selection as a process: The multiple dimensions of race in framing educational choice. *Social Problems, 46*, 418–435.

Saporito, S., & Sohoni, D. (2006). Coloring outside the lines: Racial segregation in public schools and their attendance boundaries. *Sociology of Education, 79*, 81–105.

Schneider, M., & Buckley, J. (2002). What do parents want from schools? Evidence from the Internet. *Educational Evaluation and Policy Analysis, 24*, 133–144.

Schofield, J. W., & Sagar, H. A. (1983). Desegregation, school practices, and student race relations. In C. Rossell & W. Hawley (Eds.), *The consequences of school desegregation* (pp. 58–102). Philadelphia, PA: Temple University Press.

Smrekar, C., & Honey, N. (2015). The desegregation aims and demographic contexts of magnet schools: How parents choose and why siting policies matter. *Peabody Journal of Education, 90*, 128–155.

Vervoort, M. H. M., Scholte, R. H. J., & Overbeek, G. (2010). Bullying and victimization among adolescents: The role of ethnicity and ethnic composition of school class. *Journal of Youth and Adolescence, 39*, 1–11.

Weiher, G. R., & Tedin, K. L. (2002). Does choice lead to racially distinctive schools? Charter schools and household preferences. *Journal of Policy Analysis and Management, 21*, 79–92.

Chapter 6

DeShaney v. Winnebago, 489 U.S. 189 (1989).
Fisher v. the University of Texas at Austin (Fisher I), 133 S.Ct. 2411 (2013).
Fisher v. the University of Texas at Austin (Fisher II), No. 14–981 (June 23, 2016).
Grutter v. Bollinger, 539 U.S. 306 (2003).
Levesque, R. J. R. (2008). *Rethinking child maltreatment law: Returning to first principles*. New York, NY: Springer.
Levesque, R. J. R. (2014). Discrimination, developmental science, and the law: Addressing dramatic shifts in civil rights jurisprudence. *American Journal of Orthopsychiatry, 84*, 25–34.
Levesque, R. J. R. (2015). *Adolescence, discrimination, and the law: Addressing dramatic shifts in equality jurisprudence*. New York, NY: New York University Press.
Parents Involved in Community Schools v. Seattle School District No. 1, 127 S. Ct. 2738 (2007).
Reardon, S. F., & Owens, A. (2014). 60 years after *Brown*: Trends and consequences of school segregation. *Annual Review of Sociology, 40*, 199–218.
US Government Accountability Office. (2016). *K–12 education: Better use of information could help agencies identify disparities and address racial discrimination*. Washington, DC: Author.

About the Author

Roger J.R. Levesque, J.D., Ph.D., is a professor of criminal justice in the College of Arts and Sciences at Indiana University and professor of law at Maurer School of Law. He is Editor-in-Chief of the *Journal of Youth and Adolescence* as well as *Adolescent Research Review.* He is an award-winning author of more than a dozen books, most recently *Adolescents, Discrimination, and the Law* (2015) and *Adolescence, Privacy, and the Law: A Developmental Science Perspective* (2016).

Index

Page numbers followed by *f* indicate figures; *t* indicate tables.

www.ingramcontent.com/pod-product-compliance
Ingram Content Group UK Ltd.
Pitfield, Milton Keynes, MK11 3LW, UK
UKHW022024150926
475595UK00013B/268

9 780190 633639